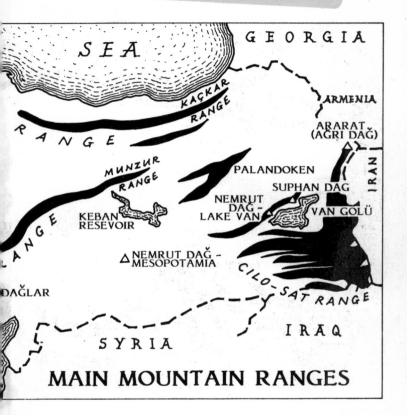

MAIN MOUNTAIN RANGES

THE MOUNTAINS OF TURKEY

The cliffs of Eski Kâhta, on the route to Nemrut Dağ (upper Mesopotamia)
(see p167)

THE MOUNTAINS OF TURKEY

by

KARL SMITH

CICERONE PRESS
MILNTHORPE, CUMBRIA

A catalogue record for this book is available from the British Library

ACKNOWLEDGEMENTS

Without the help and encouragement of several people, this book would have been slimmer, taken longer to write, or possibly not exist. Firstly, I would like to thank my friend Tim Collins, a Turkophile whose enthusiasm for the country originally inspired me to visit. His help with the natural history notes is also much appreciated - Tim provided me with all the birdwatching notes. Also to the people who have accompanied me on several visits - Cathy Woodhead (who lent several photographs for publication), Joshua and Jonathan Goldstein and others.

The Gurbuz brothers, Fikret and Ahmed, of Trek Travel, generously helped me in the Kaçkar and Aladağlar, as did numerous members of their crew, particularly Ismail Altınay in the Kaçkar and Ramazan Akpınar and family in the Aladağlar.

To Karel and Helen Winterink, from Amsterdam, who sent me the maps, sorry I lost your address, but thanks.

Thanks to Allan Smith for drawing the Kaçkar maps at short notice, and to George Heydon for proofreading the introductory chapters. Thanks to John Edmondson for further advice on the text, and to John Newton for the Mount Ararat photograph.

Sirali Aydın, Mevlut Yıldırım, Cemil Albayrak, Akın, Halil Meydan, and Enver Kibar, thanks also for making my stay in Yusufeli such an enjoyable one.

Finally, a big thank you to all the Turkish people, whose names I never knew, whose unfailing kindness and hospitality encouraged me to keep returning year after year.

Front Cover: Direktas

CONTENTS

5

ADVICE TO READERS

Readers are advised that whilst every effort is taken by the author to ensure the accuracy of this guidebook, changes can occur which may affect the contents. It is advisable to check locally on transport, accommodation, shops etc. but even rights of way can be altered, and more especially overseas, paths can be eradicated by landslip, forest fires or changes of ownership. The publisher would welcome notes of any such changes

PREFACE

Mention Turkey as a holiday destination to most people and they will think of sandy beaches and the crystal clear waters of the Mediterranean. The more informed may conjure up images of the minarets of Istanbul and rock churches in Cappadocia. Mention the country to a walker or climber, and they will likely think of Mount Ararat.

Both perceptions represent a widely-held ignorance of what this vast country has to offer. A thousand miles across, it has a remarkable variety of landscapes and cultures. For the climber, there are mountain chains of dramatic snow-capped peaks, and isolated volcanoes over 4000m high, most of which are seldom visited. There is scope for a dozen or more guidebooks to these mountains; this one volume can only hope to awaken peoples' awareness, and encourage them to discover the delights on offer themselves.

This book is aimed at both trekkers and peak-baggers. To this end, descriptions of the easiest means of ascent of most major Turkish mountains have been included. Thus, it is not a climbing guide so much as a scrambler's guide. There are very few routes described in this book on which a competent scrambler would feel a rope is necessary.

The UIAA grading scheme is used for routes to summits; where a route does not have a grade, this is because it is easy walking.

I have been back to Turkey for several extended trips since my first visit, and writing this book brings back memories of great days spent walking there. Foremost amongst these were the weeks in the Kaçkar mountains, where for once the sun did shine every day, scrambling up to summits that appeared in no books, and were rarely trodden by anyone other than Turks; frequently, I wasn't even able to discover the name until much later.

Anyone prepared to take the time and effort to go off the beaten track will find similar rewards there for the taking. There are several points in the text where ignorance is confessed and an untried itinerary suggested. Entering uncharted territory as it does, it is felt better to mention possibilities than ignore them. Use your judgement and sense of adventure and you may find yourself, like me, looking forward to the next visit.

Subsequent editions of this book rely on feedback from readers; I am always interested in hearing from others who have been to Turkey and explored areas only touched upon in the text. I can be contacted via the publishers: Cicerone Press, 2 Police Square, Milnthorpe, Cumbria LA7 7PY.

Border post, Turkey. Mt Ararat and Little Ararat behind. Photo: J Newton

PART ONE

Introduction

History and people

Human settlement in Anatolia dates back to 7500 BC, when a flourishing town developed at Çatal Hüyük, near modern Konya - one of the earliest recorded settlements on earth. The culture there was remarkably advanced, with rich pottery and sculpture artefacts having been found during excavations.

It was not until the Bronze Age (2600 BC onwards) however, that the first of Turkey's great empires, the Hittite empire, began to develop. Alaca Höyük, east of Ankara, was the one of the first important cities belonging to the Hatti, predecessors of the Hittites proper, who established their rule around 1600 BC. The new Hittite capital was at Hattuşaş, near Alaca Höyük. Remains can still be seen of this magnificent site, and it is well worth a visit.

At its height, the Hittite empire covered most of Anatolia and Syria. Its subsequent decline led to a more complex pattern of cultures and states. From the West, Phrygians entered Anatolia, and Greeks settled along the Aegean and Mediterranean coasts. These became separate kingdoms, from Ionia in the west through Lycia to Pamphylia in the east. Simultaneously, a great civilisation developed around Lake Van. Little is known of the Urartians, who had their capital on the outskirts of modern-day Van.

It would be hard to over-emphasise the importance of the coastal cities in the development of the ancient Greek, and hence western, world. Many of the great writers, philosophers and artists of the ancient world came from here - mainland Greece was, in the early stages of Hellenic culture, of minor significance.

The Persians ended this dominance when they invaded Anatolia, and held the land until Alexander the Great crossed the Dardanelles in 334 BC and went on to capture much of the Near East. After his death, much of the country reverted into small, warring city states, and this remained the position until the Romans colonised Anatolia.

They were to have a profound effect on the country, and many of their buildings are still visible today. The Emperor Constantine developed the ancient Byzantium into the city which bore his name until very recently. His successor, Justinian, left us with one of the greatest of all buildings - Hagia (Aya) Sofia.

As the Roman empire crumbled, Constantinople flourished and became the seat of the Byzantine empire and the Orthodox church. The Byzantine empire continued for 1000 years, but its death knell was sounded by Islamic invaders from the East. Coming in several waves, the first of these were the Seljuks. Originating from Central Asia in what is now Chinese Turkestan, these are of the same stock as modern day Turks. The Seljuks gained control of most of Anatolia, though not Constantinople, and ruled from Iznik. The Byzantine empire suffered further depredation at the hands of supposedly friendly Christian Crusaders, and Constantinople was finally captured in 1453 by the next wave of Turkish invaders, the Ottomans.

Constantinople, re-named Istanbul, became the centre of the new Ottoman empire, and received the many beautiful mosques which are such a feature of the city today. At its height, the Ottoman Empire controlled much of Eastern Europe and threatened the West. Decline set in, however, and by the end of the nineteenth century Turkey had lost its influence and become the "sick man" of Europe.

The early years of this century saw great unrest, with the "Young Turks" deposing the Sultan and seizing power. World War One left the Turks defeated, having sided with Germany, and in the aftermath it appeared that Turkey was likely to disintegrate as a country. That it still exists is largely due to the influence of one man - Mustafa Kemal Ataturk. A War of Independence ensued, in which Ataturk as military leader was victorious, and the Turkish Republic came into existence in 1923.

At this time, there was a great transfer of population between Greece and Turkey. Greeks, who had been living in Anatolia since Hellenic times, were uprooted and moved to modern-day Greece. Cities such as Istanbul and Izmir had very large Greek populations, but also the Greek influence is still to be seen in some of the fine houses of the Black Sea region, or of the villages of Cappadocia.

Important as his victory was, Ataturk was as influential in his subsequent social reforms. Turkey became a secular state, a modified Roman alphabet was adopted and the old Arabic one scrapped, everything from the fez to polygamy was banned, and Turkey generally became much more westernised.

Subsequent history has not been easy, with a series of military coups occurring from 1960 to 1980. Despite economic problems and continued Kurdish unrest in the South-east, Turkey has managed to become much more affluent and industrialised in the last decade, to the extent that it wishes to become a member of the EEC.

Currently Turkey's population is 97% Muslim. There are several small Orthodox Christian communities remaining, primarily in Istanbul. A small, fascinating pocket of Christianity is found in the south of the country, near Midyat and Mardin. At one time the seat of the Syrian Patriarch, the monastery of Der Zafferan, though sadly in decline, still holds services in the Aramaic language.

Most of Turkey's population are ethnic Turks. The largest minority group are the Kurds. Recent years has seen the emergence of a Kurdish separatist movement and the south-east corner of Turkey is unsafe for travellers to visit - see relevant section below.

Of the ethnic Turks, there are still one or two groups amongst them who have maintained a distinct identity. Of these, the trekker is most likely to encounter the Yoruk people. Originally nomadic, they now live the typical high mountain life of migration between summer pastures and winter lowlands. The inhabitants of Yedigöller, in the Aladağlar, are Yoruk. The Black Sea coastal region has its own distinctive mix of people, which is discussed more fully in the Kaçkar Mountains chapter.

Flora and fauna

The diverse climates and its geographical location between two continents has given Turkey a rich flora and fauna. A detailed description of Turkey's flora is beyond the scope of this book, but for anyone interested I would recommend Oleg Polunin's guide to the flora of the region. This field guide provides comprehensive coverage, including details on the many rarities and endemic species.

The Central Anatolian plateau consists primarily of arid grasslands, but with several large lakes and marsh areas of great interest to the naturalist, such as the Sultan sazlık marshes south of Kayseri. Bordering the region to the north, the Pontic range stretches from the far eastern part of the country to the Bosphorus. Mainly wooded with fir, the relatively damp climate supports a typically sub-alpine flora. In places such as the Kaçkar where the mountains attain greater height, a true alpine flora occurs. These mountains are particularly famous for their azaleas (Azalea ponticum) and rhododendron. The flora there is covered in greater detail in the introduction to the Kaçkar section.

The southern reaches of the Anatolian plateau rise to the Taurus chain, which descends steeply to the Mediterranean coast in the west, and the upper Mesopotamian plain in the east. The more arid climate and predominant limestone combine to create a typically Mediterranean mountain flora of black pine thinning to karstic alpine grassland. It is in such places that many of Turkey's great rarities are found, including several endemic species. There has sadly been a large illicit trade in rare orchids and crocuses in recent years from this area.

Despite the popularity of hunting, and the gradual erosion of habitat by more intensive forms of agriculture, the Turkish countryside, particularly in the mountains, still manages to support a considerable amount of wildlife. Of the larger mammals, brown bears are the most spectacular. These are still to be found in reasonable numbers in the Cilo Sat range and in the Kaçkar mountains. Unfortunately they appear to receive no legal protection, and hunters from overseas, particularly the United States, pay large sums for the privilege of shooting them. This deplorable situation seems likely to result in their ultimate extinction unless controlled.

Wolves cover much of mountain Turkey, although are extremely secretive. More common is the jackal. In the high mountains, ibex and chamois are occasionally visible in the remote cwms. Again, these are heavily hunted. Of the smaller mammals, the red squirrel still thrives in the Kaçkar mountains, and makes an attractive sight.

Turkey's position as a crossroads means that it has a particularly rich bird population. As most readers of this book will be visiting the country outside the migration season, I shall concentrate on the resident species.

Of the raptors, golden eagles are widespread, and abundant in some mountain locations. Four species of vultures occur - griffon, black, Egyptian and lammergeier. The latter can sometimes be seen near the summits of the Ala Dağ and Kaçkar peaks.

In pine forests on lower slopes, Kruper's nuthatch are often noticed by their loud, insistent calls. At or above treeline, the diminutive red-fronted serin is often abundant. In gorges and around cliffs, Alpine swifts and crag martins are quite common. Also in rocky areas, the blue rock thrush and wallcreeper are sometimes seen. The latter, with its distinctive black and red wings and butterfly-like flight, occurs at great heights and can sometimes be found on the very summits of the high mountains.

On the stony alpine meadows and sparsely vegetated slopes are found rock thrush, crimson-winged finch, shorelark and snowfinch. At certain times of the year the finches occur in large flocks, which are best observed as they come to drink from a water source during the heat of the day. Also found in these areas, but harder to see, are black redstart, Radde's and Alpine accentors. Choughs and Alpine choughs are common at high altitude, and ravens are scarce but widespread in the same habitat.

One of the prize sights is the Caspian snowcock. This large, pale bird with distinctive white markings can be found in the higher cwms of both the Ala Dağ and Kaçkar Mountains; its flight is very low and fast. The much scarcer Caucasian black grouse is restricted to the Kackar mountains, where it occurs near rhododendron scrub and alpine meadows.

In Eastern Turkey, the Lake Van area holds several interesting species. The crater lake of Nemrut Dağ has a relic population of velvet scoter, while on the slopes of this and neighbouring peaks are found grey-necked bunting, red-tailed wheatear and cinereous bunting.

Climate - when to visit

To describe the climate, it is best to split the country into five broad regions: the Mediterranean coast; central and eastern Anatolia; the

Black Sea region; the Taurus mountains and the Southeast plains.

Of these regions, the first is by far the mildest. Winters in the Mediterranean and Aegean are usually mild, but with frequent cold fronts arriving, bringing wet weather. In summer, the temperatures along the southern coast can rise to an unpleasant 40 C. Spring and autumn are ideal times to visit, although there is the risk of unsettled weather then. Central and eastern Anatolia, covering the Lake Van and Ararat areas, as well as Erciyes Dağ, is much more continental in climate. Summers tend to be dry, but cooler in the east than in central Anatolia, owing to the higher altitude of the plateau (around 1500m on average in central Anatolia, rising to 2000m in the east). The only practical time to visit is summer if climbing is planned. Outside this period, the roads can be blocked with snow, and the temperatures can fall as low as -30 C.

The Black Sea region is much wetter than the rest of Turkey, and for much of the year the mountains are shrouded in mists. In winter, the heavy precipitation occurs as snow, creating avalanche risk in the Kaçkar range. The best time to visit the region is in July and August. Any earlier, and the winter snows will not have receded sufficiently to allow passage over the high cols. The high yaylas, one of the main attractions of the region, are often not occupied until mid or late July. After late August, the weather starts to close in and the yaylas are abandoned before the first snow of winter.

The Taurus mountains have a longer season for the trekker than the Kaçkar, being more arid and further south. Winters here are also very cold, with considerable snowfall (the Aladağlar are a skiing area). There are many beautiful clear days at this time of year, when climbing whilst in the sun feels warm. The heavy snow cover makes the region ideal for ski-touring. Perhaps June is the ideal month for physical walking conditions - not too hot, long days and plenty of snow covering the screes. The only disadvantage is that some of the higher yaylas may not be occupied - for this, the trekker must wait until early July.

By late July and early August, the weather, though settled, can get very hot on the lower slopes. Whilst this is frequently tolerable, a major problem is the shortage of water as the small lakes and springs dry up the Aladağlar are best avoided in August.

The final area, the upper Mesopotamian plain in the south of Turkey, is only represented in this book by the walk to Nemrut Dağ. This hike is manageable throughout the year, although winter can be very cold, and very hot (though bearable) in summer. The climate is very arid, and extremely hot in summer down on the plains - temperatures near the Syrian border can reach 50 C.

Getting there

Turkey is well served by international airlines, the major airports being Istanbul and Ankara. The former has more flights, whilst the latter is closer to the trekking areas. Turkey's recent tourist boom has led to charter flights operating between Europe and some of the coastal airports: Izmir, Dalaman (near Fethiye), and Antalya. Of these, Antalya is best located for trekking purposes, whilst Dalaman is the most out-of-the-way. A charter flight offers probably the cheapest and most practical method of getting to Turkey.

Overland, Turkey is accessible by road from Greece and Bulgaria. The old "magic bus" to Istanbul still operates in some guise or other, and this provides a cheap, if time-consuming and uncomfortable, means of getting there. If time is limited, though, a charter flight makes more sense. The buses generally pass through Munich, and offer transport to returning guest workers in Germany.

There is a bus between Athens and Istanbul, via Thessaloniki, daily, and this offers a cheap and efficient means of getting there. The train between Athens and Istanbul offers the sole attraction of being able to travel free if you are in possession of an Interrail pass. Otherwise, it is far too slow to justify taking it in preference to the bus. The Orient Express used to run through Belgrade, although with the recent war in Yugoslavia, this may have altered. Despite the romantic image, this is a rather ordinary train nowadays, and offers few advantages as a means of reaching the country.

By sea

Turkey can be reached from several points by sea. There is a car ferry which departs Venice, via Piraeus, weekly on a Saturday, arriving Istanbul on Tuesday. Turkish maritime lines also operate a similar ferry from Venice to Izmir, departing Saturday and arriving Tuesday.

From Greece there are several ferries plying between the Greek Islands and the Turkish mainland. Despite the short distance, prices are unreasonably high. The ferries are as follows:

Lesbos to Ayvalık; Chios to Çeşme; Samos to Kuşadaşı; Kos to Bodrum; Rhodes to Marmaris.

Whilst arriving in Turkey by sea from Greece may seem romantic, it is worth pointing out a major drawback. Under Greek law, you are **not permitted** to enter Turkey if you have arrived in Greece by charter flight. The reasons for this are the enmity between Greek and Turkish governments, together with an understandable desire to protect the Greeks' own tourist industry.

Driving into Turkey

If you are planning to visit for any length of time, you might consider driving to Turkey. It is important to check that your green card insurance is valid for the whole of Turkey, not just the (small) European part. On entering Turkey, you as the driver will have the details of the car stamped on your passport, and it is important when you leave the country that you are driving the same vehicle, otherwise you will be liable for import duty on the vehicle.

Transport within Turkey

Buses

Fortunately for the traveller, Turkey has an excellent bus service. Every town or large village, no matter how remote, generally has at least one bus a day to it. Turkey is still a developing country, and most of the inhabitants cannot afford a car - consequently, the buses are the main form of transport. The network is mainly privately operated, although many towns operate their own local services.

The larger cities generally have several buses a day running between them, up to several hundred a day on the popular routes such as Ankara - Istanbul. The network is so good, in fact, that it is questionable as to whether there is any point in having your own car transport as a tourist in Turkey. The prices are extremely cheap. When I first visited the country, £4 would get you from Istanbul to Erzerum in the east, and £10 would get you halfway across the continent to Tehran. Whilst prices have risen, the buses still offer extraordinary value for money. An indication of prices and times for buses is given below:

Istanbul -	Ankara	8hrs	£8 to £10
Istanbul -	Ankara - Kayseri	13hrs	£12.50
Istanbul -	Erzurum	22hrs	£16
Istanbul -	Trabzon	24hrs	£18
Kayseri -	Sivas	3hrs	£2
Kayseri -	Sivas - Erzurum	11hrs	£7
Kayseri -	Nigde	1hr 30mins	£1.70
Erzurum -	Trabzon	7hrs	£7

Minibuses and Dolmuşes

Complementing the bus network is an excellent minibus system, although it often frustrates the first-time visitor. Minibuses, generally Ford Transits or similar, operate wherever there is insufficient traffic to justify a large bus. They are usually slower and slightly more expensive than a bus. In the cities the true "Dolmuş" operates, a Turkish institution. These are minibuses (or large old American cars in Istanbul) which operate on a fixed route, waiting until they have enough passengers before they set off, dropping and picking up people as they go along.

The minibuses which operate between towns and villages generally have more fixed departure times, but you often find yourself waiting an extra hour or two whilst the driver hangs on for more custom. In these circumstances, it's best just to sit, drink tea, and relax. Western ideas of timekeeping simply don't apply. Prices for journeys are fixed - don't haggle.

Taxis

These represent exceptional value for money, especially if you are sharing, and are ideal for getting to those out-of-the-way places. All towns have taxis, and drivers are usually happy to wait all day whilst you do whatever you want to do. Negotiate the price beforehand.

Trains

Although it is possible to cross Turkey from west to east by train, don't plan on doing this unless you have plenty of time. Trains in Turkey (with a few notable exceptions) are generally slower, but cheaper, than buses. The express *(ekspres)* trains belie their name, and local *(yolcu* and *posta)* trains are to be avoided unless you want to spend hours stationary or being shunted backwards for no apparent reason. The exceptions are the lines between Istanbul and Ankara or Izmir. The Mavi Tren (Blue Train) is a fast, comfortable train with excellent dining and sleeping facilities. Although more expensive than the bus, it's a stylish way to travel. You need to reserve seats and sleeping accommodation on these trains by going to the station beforehand. The Istanbul departure point is from Haydarpaşa, on the Asian side of the Bosphorus - catch a ferry over to it.

Internal flights
These are fairly cheap and frequent. If you fly into Istanbul, have limited time, and are heading east, it is worth thinking about flying one way at least. There are daily flights to Erzurum, Adana and Trabzon, two or three a week to Kayseri. Typical prices are (one way):

Istanbul -	Adana	£55
Istanbul -	Erzurum	£52
Istanbul -	Trabzon	£55

Hiring a car
Car hire is expensive in Turkey. The poor roads shorten life expectancy (of both car and driver!), and big distances mean you often pay a mileage surcharge. If hiring, check carefully that you have unlimited mileage, or if not, what the surcharge rate is. This could add considerably to your bill. Basic rate, without unlimited mileage, can be from £200 to 250 a week. All the major hire car companies (Hertz, Avis etc.) are represented here, and usually have offices at the airport (see useful addresses). Local hirers are quite a bit cheaper. The advantage of having your own car is being able to stop at the fascinating ruins or old caravanserais that buses shoot past - the disadvantage being driving on some of the most accident-prone roads anywhere.

Ferries

Several Turkish Maritime Lines (TML) ferries operate along the coast from Istanbul, but for users of this book there is only one of any relevance. This is the Istanbul - Trabzon ferry.

This departs Istanbul every Monday (17.30), arriving Trabzon Wednesday morning. It returns from Trabzon Wednesday (22.00), arriving back in Istanbul Friday morning. It's a lovely way to end a holiday in the Kaçkar mountains, and the best way to arrive in Istanbul.

Visas

Until recently, visitors from the UK did not need visas to visit Turkey. However they are now compulsory. Fortunately, they are available on arrival in Turkey upon payment of a £5 note - travellers' cheques etc. will not do. Other nationalities should check with the Turkish Embassy or Consulate in their home country.

Changing money

Most small towns have banks, so changing money should, in theory, be fairly easy. The Turkish Lira is freely floating, and there is no black market exchange. Other than a small amount, I would recommend changing money into lira in Turkey; most UK currency exchanges don't carry lira, and offer a poor rate.

Travellers' cheques can be changed at banks in major cities, but you may encounter problems changing them elsewhere. Choose a familiar brand such as Thomas Cook Travellers Cheques. Even this is not a guarantee of success - I tried a bank in a small town in the east with a "Thomas Cook Travellers Cheques" sign on the door, only to be told it was impossible.

Credit cards can be used in large hotels, carpet shops, airlines, etc. but the users of this book are unlikely to be using such facilities throughout their holiday.

Effectively, the only means of avoiding these difficulties is to take cash. Having struggled with travellers cheques in the past, on all subsequent trips I have simply used sterling notes. Turkey is such an extremely safe country that the risk of theft is negligible, and the notes are acceptable in the most out-of-the-way places. In fact,

I quickly discovered that you don't need to wait until the banks open - just ask around in any cafe, and you will find someone who is willing to change sterling, Deutschmarks, or whatever, for lira. A copy of the latest daily paper is sent for, the current exchange rate checked, and the deal is done, with no commission charges or delay.

A word about prices in this book. Turkey suffers from chronic inflation, and what cost 1000 lire last year might cost 6,000 lire now. Consequently, I have given all prices in their pounds sterling equivalent. Despite the high inflation, the exchange rate appears to offset this, so Turkey remains a very cheap venue for the western visitor.

Health

Turkey's rapid development and industrialisation have seen a corresponding improvement in public hygiene. As a result the country is a good deal safer than most other West Asian countries. Water in towns and cities is safe to drink, if somewhat over-chlorinated. The same cannot be said of the villages, and anyone using this book is likely to be travelling through places with very basic hygiene. This, and the change of diet, mean diarrhoea is often experienced during the early stages of a holiday. It is worthwhile bringing some remedy with you eg. Immodium. Combined with the heat, diarrhoea can lead to dehydration, so carry a few sachets of rehydrating salts such as Dioralyte.

There is also a risk of contacting hepatitis, and a gamma globulin injection prior to departure is strongly recommended. Again, this risk is certainly not as high as in Third World countries.

Malaria still exists in certain areas of Southern Turkey during the summer months. These areas are principally the lower Tigris and Euphrates valleys and the Çukurova near Adana. This book does not describe walks in these areas, although someone approaching the Aladağlar from Adana side should be wary of visiting the Çukurova. Worldwide, malaria is on the increase, and resistant strains are developing. It is worth checking for up-to-the-minute health information prior to departure if visiting the Adana area.

As regards visible health risks, snakes occur in Turkey, but it is quite easy to spend a whole holiday without seeing one. There are several species of viper which have a poisonous bite; seek medical attention urgently. Scorpions also occur infrequently - be careful when overturning stones.

It is easy to exaggerate the risk of illness in Turkey- I have met very few people unfortunate enough to be ill. Beyond the above, there are the usual health precautions to take whilst in the mountains. Unless water is clearly from a spring, ensure that it is sterilised before drinking. There is a risk of Ghiardia from both domestic and wild animals having polluted the water source above you. In general, the high mountain lakes of the Kaçkar are safe to drink from.

The solar radiation is extremely intense - remember, this is much further south than the Alps. Factor 15 suncream should be carried as a matter of course. Take particular care when it is misty, as it often is in the Kaçkar; I speak from personal experience.

Altitude sickness is a distinct possibility, although in its acute form is unlikely. Headaches, listlessness and loss of appetite are frequently experienced by Ararat summiteers. Remember, the cure for altitude sickness is to get down quickly. It is not serious except in its acute form, which rarely develops below 3600m. The symptoms of Acute Mountain Sickness (AMS) are initially the same as for normal altitude sickness, but if ignored can lead to coma and death. If the person faints or shows any signs of irrational behaviour, lose altitude *immediately*.

Other hazards

The principal hazard a trekker may encounter is dogs. Most flocks of sheep are guarded by Anatolian mastiffs, large dogs bred for defending the sheep against wolf attack. One of these dogs, barking at you and with a spiked collar round its neck, can be a fearsome sight. The answer is to avoid getting between the dog and its flock. If there is a shepherd around, try to make sure he is aware of your presence in order to control the dogs. There are often several dogs guarding one flock.

A hazard peculiar to the Kaçkar are the bulls which are kept in the high pastures. If you encounter one of these, my only advice is to keep your fingers crossed.

As regards human hazards, theft is virtually unknown. The only instances of theft I have heard of have been in the far eastern part of the country, particularly on Mount Ararat. Frequently I have left my belongings, including camera and wallet, on the bus at a rest stop in the safe knowledge that it will be there on my return. At other times I have left a large rucksack on a bench somewhere whilst I went off shopping for half an hour. Whilst this may change one day, it is true to say that your belongings are as safe in Turkey as in any country.

A few years ago, English newspapers carried reports of a climber who had been shot by a Kurd for entering his house whilst the man's wife was present and he absent. Such incidents are mercifully extremely rare, but it is worth bearing in mind that the concept of honour differs in the strongly traditional East of Turkey from that in the West. See "etiquette" section to avoid making the same mistake!

As previously mentioned, there has been a long-running conflict between the Turkish authorities and the Kurdish PKK. This has become noticeably worse over the past few years, and is spreading both in geographical area and in intensity. The Cilo Sat range has been closed to outside visitors for a number of years, and seems likely to remain so for a long time to come. More worrying has been the extension of guerrilla activity to the Lake Van area, with several tourists having been kidnapped recently. At the time of writing, the South-east of Turkey has been declared by the British Foreign Office an area that is unsafe to visit. Anyone planning to visit one of the following areas should check with the embassy prior to departure:

> Munzur range
> Lake Van area
> Mount Ararat area
> Cilo Sat range
> (possibly) Nemrut Dağ (near Kahta)

Outside the Kurdish areas, there is virtually no risk to travellers whatsoever. The risk should be put in its proper perspective. A visitor to Turkey is infinitely safer than, say, a tourist in Miami or New York, and it would be a great pity if you were to miss the splendours of Turkey because of trouble in isolated areas. Turkey is vast - the Kaçkar or Ala Dağ mountains are an equivalent distance from the troubled South-east as Paris is from Belfast.

Medical and rescue facilities

Turkey has quite a good network of rural health centres, found in most small towns and the larger villages. These can treat most minor complaints, have essential medicines such as antibiotics, and are usually staffed by qualified doctors. Turkey has an admirable policy of sending newly-qualified doctors to work in far-flung regions - visit a health centre in the Kaçkar or Ala Dağ and the doctor is likely to be from Istanbul or Ankara.

For more serious injuries, it is necessary to evacuate the casualty to a large town or city. In such circumstances, formal rescue facilities are non-existent. Descend to the nearest sizeable village, and keep your eyes open for telephone cables. Bear in mind that most villages in Turkey will have some form of horse or mule transport, which can be used to evacuate the casualty. A further idea, and I can't vouch for how successful this would be, would be to contact the nearest police or army base. The Turkish army are well equipped with helicopters, and may be willing to evacuate a casualty in a crisis. Clearly, solo trekking or climbing carries some risks in an isolated area.

Maps

Good maps are virtually unobtainable in Turkey. Whilst they do exist, detailed maps are regarded as of military significance, and consequently prohibited.

For a general map of the country, the 1:1,000,000 Kummerly + Frey, ref. 01177 covers the whole country. More detailed are the two Roger Lascelles Large Scale National Maps, scale 1:800,000, Turkey, West and Turkey, East.

For maps of the mountains, Dr Bozkurt Ergor of the Turkish Mountaineering Federation (TDF - see useful addresses) has been preparing the definitive series, covering all the major ranges and mountains at 1:25,000 scale. These are not yet in print, although maps based on them seem to circulate freely - the copyright of many Turkish maps seems open to dispute. It is worth contacting the TDF to see what the current situation is, but, failing this, the best maps readily available are those produced by Trek Travel. They print small maps to the Kaçkar, Aladağlar, and Ararat. Fikret Gurbuz, a Director of Trek Travel told me that he had been heavily fined by the Turkish authorities for producing the maps. Whilst printed for the benefit of their trekking clients, it may be possible to come to some arrangement whereby you get hold of one of the maps.

Trekking supplies

Food suitable for backpacking is surprisingly easy to come by. Apart from the abundant fresh fruit and vegetables, of which Turkey is a major producer, Turkey has a developed food packaging industry.

Dried pasta (*makarna*) is available in all towns, as are packet soups. For something more appetising, Turkish sheep - or goat's milk cheese (*beyaz peynir*) is cheap and lasts well, though it needs wrapping in a waterproof plastic bag. Dried nuts and fruit are a feature of many a street corner vendor's stall.

Turkish people have a very sweet tooth, and there is an abundance of sweets for sale everywhere. More nutritious, halva is made from crushed sesame seeds and is worth trying if you haven't already done so. A speciality of Gumuşhane, but more widely available, is *pestil*. This consists of long, very thin sheets of dried apricot pulp, often flavoured with spices or nuts.

On trek in the mountains, provisions are a lot harder to come by. The very thin sheets of dry bread, yufka, take some getting used to, but have a shelf life of two years! Other than this, it is largely pot luck as to what you will find in remote areas. Where food is commonly available, I have mentioned it in the relevant area description.

In summary, unless you have a craving for some particular delicacy, there is little point in carrying food out to Turkey with you. Fuel for stoves is more of a problem. Ideally, a stove that runs on methylated spirits (*ispirto*) or petrol (*petrol*) should be brought. Items such as camping gaz cylinders and Coleman fuel are to all intents and purposes unobtainable in Turkey.

Turkey does not have a developed trekking culture, and consequently items of kit such as tents, sleeping bags or rucksacks are not available. Besides obviously bringing your own, it is worth thinking about carrying a small repair kit if you are out in Turkey for any length of time.

Etiquette

As a foreigner and *misafir* (honoured guest), you will undoubtedly be invited into someone's home at some stage. You will not be expected to behave as impeccably as a fellow Turk would, but it is nice to avoid faux pas where possible. On entering the house, take off your shoes. You will sometimes be given plastic slippers to put on. If invited to eat, the males of the household will eat with you, whilst the women stay in the kitchen and bring the food in. It is in order for western women to eat with the males, and expected. Chances are, you will be sat around a low table, and offered more to eat than you can possibly manage - it is quite in order to say when you have had your fill. One final point - it is considered impolite to have the soles of your feet visible or pointing towards other people.

As mentioned in the Hazards section, it is wise to avoid offending the code of honour prevalent in the more traditional east of the country. It is pointless in a book of this nature to reflect on the subjugation of women in Turkey; it is simply worth pointing out that the traveller needs to tread warily. Entering a house with women inside is not accepted unless invited to do so by a male householder. Likewise, many women do not like having their photographs taken, and it is diplomatic to refrain from doing so if they make their objections known.

It may seem from some of the above that Turkey is not a suitable destination for women travellers. This is far from the truth, as countless women who have been there will testify. However, the single woman traveller can expect some unwelcome advances from local males. The generally accepted advice is to ignore them totally. This is deemed preferable to verbally abusing the man - justified or tempting this may be, but this is still a male-dominated society where a slight from a woman is not readily accepted.

Turkish mountaineering organisations

Mountaineering and walking is still something of a rarity in Turkey

- until recently, it was virtually unheard of as a recreational activity. In one town I visited, Manisa, there was a local man who frequently walked up Mount Spiliyous. He was dubbed "the Tarzan of Manisa" for this eccentricity. The situation has changed, and several mountaineering clubs now exist, most of which are either university clubs or branches of the Turkish Mountaineering Federation (TDF, Turkiye Dağcılık Federasyonu).

This is the official organisation for representing mountaineering, sponsored by the government. Like many such august institutions, it is not particularly attuned to the wants of active mountaineers and hikers. One of its principal roles is that of licensing qualified guides; lists of such guides can be provided upon request.

A more active organisation is the Anatolian Mountaineers Union (ADB, Anadolu Dağcılar Birligi). Based in Ankara, it produces a useful newsletter (in Turkish), and can put you in touch with like-minded Turks who have detailed regional knowledge. A useful regional club is the Kayseri Mountaineering Club (KDK Kayseri Dağcılık Kulubu). As one might expect, they are active around the Aladağlar and Erciyes Dağ areas. Linked to the TDF, the KDK is also a club for professional guides. It can be contacted via one of their members, Tekin Kuçuknalbant (see useful addresses).

There are climbing clubs at Izmir University, Istanbul and Bosphorus Universities, whose members are active and have frequent trips to the Aladağlar and other ranges. Unfortunately I don't have the addresses, but it should be easy to obtain via the University and the local embassy.

Useful Addresses

General

Turkish Embassy
43 Belgrave Square
London SW1X 8PA
Tel: 0171 235 5252

Contact: Mr M.Donmez, the person to contact (as of writing) for a permit to climb Ararat. Also write if planning to visit a restricted area such as Cilo Sat.

Car hire

Avis:	Trabzon - lobby of Hotel Uşta, Tel: 031-23740
	Samsun - Lise Caddesi 241, Tel: 361-33288
Budget:	head office Tepebaşı Katlı, Otoparki Beyoglu
	80050 Istanbul, Tel: (1) 145 07 66,
	Fax: (1) 149 15 14
	- numerous branches throughout western Turkey
Europcar:	head office Cumhuriyet Cad. 47/2 Taksim
	Istanbul, Tel: (1) 154 77 88, Fax: (1) 150 88 88
	- numerous branches at airports and major cities
Hertz:	central office Cumhuriyet Cad. 295, 80230
	Harbiye, Istanbul, Tel: (1) 145 07 66,
	Fax: (1) 149 15 14
	- coverage as for Europcar and Budget
Let's Rent-a-Car:	offices in Istanbul, Ankara, Izmir and Antalya,
	Tel: (1) 573 45 02, (1) 573 29 20

Turkish mountaineering organisations

TDF Beden Terbiyesi Genel Müdürlüğü, Ulus İş hanı, A Blok, Ulus, Ankara, Tel: (4) 310 8566 ext. 356

ADB PO Box 750, Kızılay, Ankara, Tel: (4) 136 9476; or Bakcelievler 1 Cad. 31/4 Ankara

Trekking agencies and guides

Trek Travel, Aydede Caddesi 10 80090 taksim, Istanbul, Tel: (90-1) 155 1624
- the most experienced trek operators in Turkey. Tours to all major Turkish ranges, including Mount Ararat.

Travel Alternatif, Bagdat Cad., Samnu İş Merkezı, 36/8 81030 Kızıltoprak, Istanbul, Tel: (90-1) 345 66 50, Fax: (90-1) 348 10 53
- they run tailor-made treks to Bolkar (min. 8 persons), as well as SW Turkey, Kaçkar.

11 Tur Tourism + Trade + Enterprises Co. Ltd. Caykara Cad. 100A Erzurum, Fax/Tel: (90-011) 41515-31070
- trekking, ski-ing and canoeing in the Kaçkar region

Ala Dağ region:

Tekin Kuçuknalbant, Mete Caddesi 36/3 38010 Kayseri, Tel: (351) 13393
- a guide and member of the Kayseri Mountaineering Club (KDK).

Ali & Cavit Şafak, Pansion Çukurbağ, Bereketlı Mahallesı, 51660 Çamardi, Niğde, Tel: 4837 1420-3
- Ali acts as a guide and source of information to the region.

Kaçkar region:

Ismail Altınay, Yaylalar Köyü, Yusufeli, Artvin, Tel. 0589 4228
- a very helpful man, who runs the shop and rest-house in Yaylalar. He formerly worked for Trek Travel, and understands trekkers' needs.

Halil Meydan, Eski Çarsı no. 8, Yusufeli, Artvin
- a good source of maps. His brother, Ibrahim, is a trekking guide who speaks good English.

Mehmet Okumuş PO Box 15, Ayder, Hemşin, Pazar, Rize.
- acts as a trekking guide

Kadir Sarı, Hotel Cağlayan, Ayder, Camlıhemsin, Rize
- runs a nice hotel, and also acts as a trekking guide.

Bibliography

(AJ = Alpine Journal)

General

The Kurds and Kurdistan. D. Kinnane, London, Institute of Race
Relations, Oxford University Press.
An academic socio-historic study of the Kurds in South-east
Turkey.

The Towers of Trebizond. Rose Macaulay.
A famous work of fiction which paints a wonderful portrait of
the Eastern Black Sea region.

Black Sea. Boyut Publishing Group. Istanbul 1990.
A very informative guide to the Black Sea region.

Memed my Hawk (Turkish title - *Ince Memed*). Yashar Kemal, Collins
1961.
This and other works by Turkey's most famous author are
essential reading for anyone visiting the Anatolian countryside
and the Taurus mountains.

Turkey - a Travel Survival Kit. Tom Brosnahan 1985. Lonely Planet
Publications, Victoria.
An excellent, comprehensive guide for the general traveller,
with detailed information on towns and cities.

Flora and fauna

Flora of Turkey. Ed. P.H.Davis 1965.Edinburgh University Press 9
vols.
An academic treatise, the standard guide to Turkish flora.

Flowers of the Mediterranean. O.Polunin and A.Huxley 1967. Chatto
and Windus.
The most useful guide to Turkish flora available.

Mediterranean Wildflowers. Marjorie Blamey and Christopher Wilson
1993. Harper Collins.

Birds of Britain and Europe with North Africa and the Middle East.
Heinzel, H., Fitter, R., and Parslow J., London 1985 (revised
edition).

Birds of Europe (with North Africa and the Middle East). Lars Jonsson, Christopher Helm 1992.

Aladağlar

"Cambridge Aladağ Expedition 1965". J.Ashburner *CUMC Journal*, 1966

Turkish Taurus Expedition 1967. D.Robinson, Dept. of Physical Education, Leeds University, 1968

"Aladağ". *AJ* 54, 1943-44 p.235
This is very detailed, with a map, and gives a good feel of what exploring this range was like.

Bolkar Toros

"Bolkar Mountains". Julie Henning, *Outdoor Action*, May 1992 pp.46-48

Ararat and Lake Van area

Transcaucasia and Ararat. James Bryce 1896. Macmillan & Co. London
A brilliant book, with over 100 pages on Mt Ararat alone, and a wealth of information on Armenia and the Armenians.

"Ararat revisited". J.Town, *AJ* 89, 1984 p.145

Highlands of Asiatic Turkey. Lord Perry, late 19th century.
Information on Lake Van area.

"The Mountains of Van". Tony Arthur, *Climber and Rambler*, Dec. 1983

Report on International Climbing Meet, Mt. Ararat E Turkey February 1986. J.Town, 1986, Alpine Club Library
Useful information for anyone visiting Ararat in winter.

Cilo-Sat range

The Turkish Time Machine. Monica Jackson, Hodder and Stoughton 1966.
A book covering an expedition to the Cilo-Sat; interesting reading and worth searching out.

"Sat Dag, Hakkari". S.E.P. Nowill, *AJ* 72 p.117
   AJ 70. The expedition notes to the above.

"Cilo Dag, Sat Dag". Doug Scott, *Bulletin of Alpine Climbing Group,*
   1969 pp.17-25

"Escalades au Kurdistan". Olivier Welti, *Annales du Groupe de Haute
   Montagne,* 1969, pp.4-7

"Peaks and Passes in Kurdistan". T.Weir, *Scottish Mountaineering
   Club Journal,* 1958, pp.235-244

"Expedition to Sat Dag". *Ladies Alpine Club Journal,* 1967, pp.3-12

Western Anatolia
"Olympian Triad". *AJ* 92, 1987 p.140
   Ascents of Uludağ and Mt Olympos nr Kemer

Multi-area
"Torasan, Kackar and Mountain Rescue". S.E.P. Nowill, *AJ* 86, 1981
   p. 159
   A good source of information on approaching the Ala Dağ from
   the S.

"Climbing in Turkey". J.G.R.Harding, *Climbers' Club Journal* XV,
   1966-68 p.176
   Brief notes on the principal ranges and a detailed account of
   Erciyes Dağ.

PART TWO

The Turkish Language

If you are planning to go off the beaten track, you will need at least a few Turkish phrases. The language is unrelated to any western European language, but the people are extremely patient as you struggle to make yourself understood. It is worth taking a small phrasebook or dictionary - these are readily available in Turkey and are excellent value for money. One of the better types are the Langenscheidt Turkish/English English/Turkish dictionaries, available in a range of sizes including a small pocket-size version ideal for backpackers.

The Turkish Alphabet

Following Ataturk's reforms, Turkey abandoned Arabic script and adopted a Roman alphabet, adapted to suit the Turkish language. Fortunately for the visitor, all spelling is phonetic.

The difference between Turkish and English pronunciation of the letters and dipthongs is as follows:

a	Pronounced softly, as in the "a" in "gentleman"
c	sounds like English "j" as in "jump"
ç	pronounced "ch" as in "church"
e	"e" as in "get"
g	always hard, as in "get"
ğ	(with accent) lengthens the preceding vowel
h	is always pronounced
ı	without the dot, pronounced "uh". Sounds like the "a" in "alone"
i	pronounced "ee" as in "sheep"
j	pronounced in the French way, "zh", sounding like the "s" in "vision"

Karataş from Didvake

The summit ridge of Didvake. Peaks (l to r) : Kaçkar Dağ (far distance), Bulut Dağ, Liblin Tepe

Looking along the fine Altıparmak ridge towards Pt 3270m

o	as in "god"
ö	as French "oeu" in "oeuvre"
ş	"sh" as in "ship"
u	as in hut
ü	French "u" as in "plume"
v	after a vowel, sometimes pronounced more as a "w"]

Dipthongs:

ay	as in "buy"
ey	"ay" as in "hay"
oy	as in "ploy"
uy	like French "oui"

The last syllable is usually the one that is stressed.

General

Useful words and phrases

Hello .... *Merhaba*

Welcome .... *Hoş geldiniz*

You often hear the more formal greeting *Selamun aleykum* (peace be with you), to which the reply is *Aleykum selam* (peace be with you too)

Good morning .... *Günaydin*

Good day .... *Iyi günler*

Good evening .... *Iyi akşamlar*

Good night .... *Iyi geceler*

Goodbye (to someone remaining) .... *Allahısmarladık*

Goodbye (to someone leaving) .... *Güle güle*

Yes .... *Evet*

No .... *Hayır, Yok*

(the latter used where something isn't available, or a definite no)

Please .... *Lütfen*

Thank you .... *Mersi, Teşekkür ederim*

Okay .... *Tamam*

Numbers

1	*Bir*	20	*Yirmi*
2	*Iki*	21	*Yirmibir*
3	*Üç*	22	*Yirmiiki* etc...
4	*Dort*	30	*Otuz*
5	*Beş*	40	*Kırk*
6	*Altı*	50	*Elli*
7	*Yedi*	60	*Altmış*
8	*Sekiz*	70	*Yetmiş*
9	*Dokuz*	80	*Seksen*
10	*On*	90	*Doksan*
11	*Onbir*	100	*Yüz*
12	*Oniki* etc....	300	*Üçyüz* etc...
1000	*Bin*		
6785	*Altıbin yediyüz seksenbes*		

Asking directions

Where is....?	*.nerede?*
Where is the restaurant?	*Lokanta nerede?*

Locations and geographical terms

left	*sol*	right	*sağ*
straight ahead	*doğru*	map	*harıta*
upper	*yukarı*	lower	*aşağı*
big	*büyük*	small	*küçük*
above	*ustunde*	below	*altinda*
in front of	*onunde*	behind	*arkasında*
near	*yakın*	far	*uzak*
uphill	*yokuş*	downhill	*yokuş aşağı*
valley	*dere, vadi*	couloir	*çarşak*
river	*nehir, ırmak, suyu*	stream	*dere, çay*
lake	*göl(u)*	sea	*deniz*
snow	*kar*	glacier	*buzul*
spring	*pınar*	hot spring	*kaplıca*
waterfall(small)	*selale (caglayan)*	river source	*kaynak*
cave	*mağara*	mountain(s)	*dağ(ları)*
massif	*dağ kitlesı*	summit	*zirve*

ridge .... *sırt*	pass .... *geçidi, gedik, bel*
"narrows" .*bogaz* (lit. "throat")	gorge .... *kapuz*
main, greater (as in main	castle .... *kale*
summit) .... *başı*	rock, boulder .... *kaya*
hill .... *tepe*	stone .... *taş*
meadow .... *meydan*	upland meadow, plateau *ova*
forest .... *orman*	tree .... *ağaç*
bridge .... *kopru*	"finger" of rock (often
....	used figuratively) .... *parmak*

Colours

Black .... *kara, siyah*	white .... *ak, beyaz*
red .... *kırmızı, kızıl*	blue .... *mavi*
green .... *yeşil*	yellow .... *sarı*

An interesting explanation I was given for place names related to colour. Traditionally, certain colours represented east, west, north and south. Hence the mountain "Karataş" in the Kaçkar does not mean "black rock" but "northern rock". By the same logic, Karadeniz translates as "northern sea" rather than "Black Sea".

The colours are as follows:

north .... black *(kara)*	east .... blue *(mavi)*
south .... red *(kızıl)*	west .... white *(ak)*
	as in AkDeniz?

The weather

weather .... *hava* (also means air, wind)	
rain .... *yağmur*	snow .... *kar*
sun(ny) .... *guneş(li)*	cloud(y), mist(y) ...... *bulut(lu)*
wind .... *rüzgâr*	fog .... *şiş*
thunder .... *gök gürlemesi*	lightning .... *yıldırım*
storm .... *fırtına*	bad weather .... *bozuk*
hot .... *sicak*	cold .... *soğuk*

The time

What time is it? .... *Saat kaç?*	At what time.? ... *Saat kaçta...?*
How many hours? .... *Kaç saat?*	

35

minute ....*dakika*   hour ....*saat*
half-hour*yarım saat* (NB. *uç buçuk saat* means 3.30 - *yarım* only refers to a half-hour period, and is not used when giving the time.)
quarter-hour ....*çeyrek*   six o'clock ....*saat altı de*
It is quite crucial to get the word order correct, otherwise there will be confusion as to whether a bus, say, leaves at three o'clock (*saat uç de*) or in three hours time (*uç saat*).

now	*şimde*	later	*sonra*
morning	*sabah*	afternoon	*ikindi*
evening	*akşam*	night	*geçe*
today	*bügün*	tomorrow	*yarın*
(day before)		day after	
yesterday ....(*evvekli gün*) *düun*		tomorrow ....*yarından sonra*	

Flora and Fauna

flower	*çiçek*	sunflower	*ayçiçek*
early purple orchid (used to make a sweet drink) ....*salep*			
plane	*çinar*	mulberry tree	*düt*
fir	*koknar*	pine	*çam*
oak	*meşe*	olive tree	*zeytin*
poplar	*kavak*	willow	*söğüt*
animal	*hayvan*	bear	*ayı*
bee	*arı*	bird	*kuş*
chamois	*dağ keçisi*	deer	*geyik*
dog	*köpek*	donkey	*eşek*
goat	*keçi*	horse	*at*
mosquito	*sivrisinek*	mule	*katır*
sheep	*koyun*	sheepdog	*çobanköpeği*
snake	*yılan*	wolf	*kurt*

General trekking vocabulary

boot(s)	*postal(lar)*	compass	*pusula*
fuel	*yakut*	meths, alcohol	*ispirto*
matches	*kibrit*	sleeping bag	*uyku tulumu*
rucksack(s)	*çantar(lar)*	stove	*ocak*
tent	*çadır*		

PART THREE

Kaçkar Mountains

Introduction

Some of the most attractive mountains in Turkey, the Kaçkar are part of the range known since ancient times as the Pontic Alps. They lie in the north-eastern corner of Turkey, just inland from the Black Sea coast, and stretch from the Ovitdağ pass in the west as far eastwards as Artvin. Bounded on the east and south by the Çoruh river, the northern slopes descend steeply down to the Black Sea.

Granite and volcanic rocks predominate to form jagged peaks reminiscent of parts of central Switzerland. This impression is further re-inforced by the lush vegetation of forest and upland meadow, dotted with wooden chalets. The highest mountain is Kaçkar Dağ, 3932m, and there are several peaks over 3500m in height.

The Kaçkar range are geographically fairly simple, being points along the main watershed of the Pontic Alps. This watershed marks a dramatic climatic contrast between the dank, humid northern slopes and the arid rainshadow of the southern side.

The climatic contrasts are also mirrored culturally, with the area as a whole having probably the richest ethnic mix in the country outside the big cities.

Climate

The northern slopes of the Kaçkar mountains are by far the wettest part of Turkey. It can rain for 250 days of the year, and the annual precipitation reaches a massive 5000mm in places. At sea level this produces warm, humid conditions which allow tea and hazelnuts to be grown in large quantities. All Turkey's tea comes from here (no mean feat when you consider the amount that gets drunk), and it is the world's largest hazelnut producer.

Higher up the tea plantations give way to thick deciduous, then conifer, forest. This in turn becomes rhododendron and azalea scrub, then rich alpine pasture as height is gained.

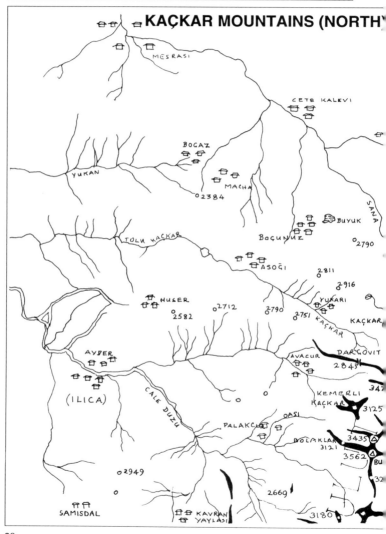

KAÇKAR MOUNTAINS (NORTH)

MESRASI

CETE KALEVI

BOGAZ

YUKAN

MACHA
○2384

TOLN KAÇKAR

BUYUK
BOÇUNUZ
SANA
○2790

ASOĞI
2811 ○

HUSER
○2582
○2712
○2790
○2751
KAÇKAR
2916 ○
YUKARI
KAÇKAR

AYDER
AVACUR
DARÇOVIT
2843

(ILICA)
ÇALE DUZU
○
○
KEMERLI
KAÇKAR
347
3125

PALAKÇA
QASI
BOLAKLAR
3435
3121
3562
Bu

○2949
○
32

2669
SAMISDAL
KAVRAN
YAYLASI
3180

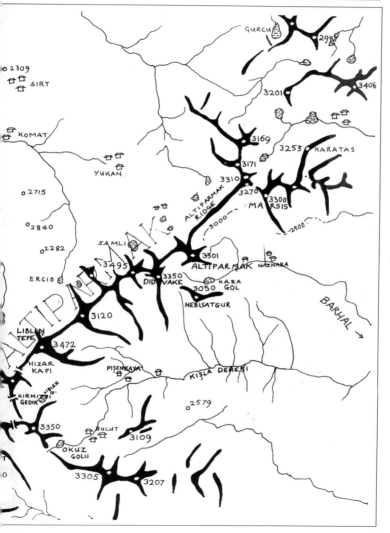

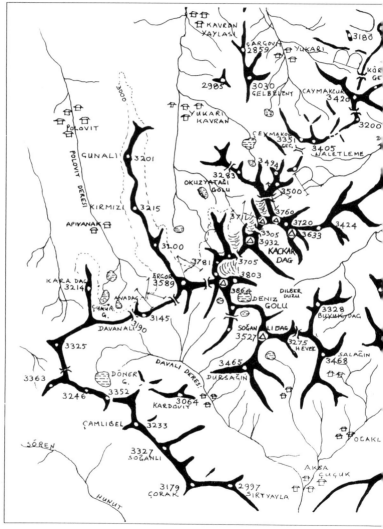

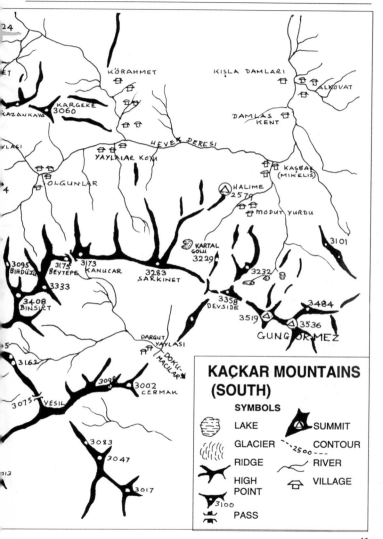

KAÇKAR MOUNTAINS
(SOUTH)

SYMBOLS

LAKE

GLACIER

RIDGE

HIGH
POINT

PASS

SUMMIT

CONTOUR

RIVER

VILLAGE

As far as the walker and climber is concerned, the single biggest factor is the ever-present mist. Humid air from the Black Sea rises and condenses, forming a dense cloud which forms by lunchtime daily. Fortunately, the mist tends to keep below 3000m, but this cannot be relied on. Add to this the dense forests and magnetic nature of the rocks, and navigational problems are bound to ensue!

In contrast, the dry southern slopes down to the Çoruh river permit olives groves and an abundance of fresh fruit, amply irrigated by the fast flowing mountain streams. Yusufeli describes itself as a "fruit paradise", and the description seems justified as you eat your way through the ripe peaches on sale at the roadside. There are even rice paddies alongside the Çoruh river.

In wintertime, the rain turns to snow which falls in abundance. The forests on the steep northern slopes are riven by avalanche trails, and on the very highest parts of the range there are still one or two residual glaciers. Travel through the area in winter can be very exhausting.

Consequently, the best time of year to visit is in July and August. Any earlier and the snow will not have melted sufficiently to allow people to return to the yaylas. Admittedly, though, if adequately equipped with axe and crampons, the mountains are delightful to climb when snow covers the scree.

From September onwards, the yaylas are deserted and the first of the winter snow appears.

Wildlife and flora

The steepness and inaccessibility of the northern slopes ensures the survival of the brown bear in one of its last Turkish strongholds. Hunted and shot by both locals and affluent American visitors, its future cannot be guaranteed. There appear sadly to be no restrictions on hunting.

Chamois, though shy, are not uncommon above the tree line, and wolves are reputed to exist here also. Ibex are scarcer than chamois, but are to be seen occasionally. An attractive sight are the red squirrels found on both sides of the range.

Of the birds, the most characteristic of the high mountains is the Caspian snowcock. Large, ptarmigan-like birds, when surprised they take off explosively and fly downhill in a low, fast manner. Other birds characteristic of this region include: red-fronted serin; lammergeier; wallcreeper; chough; rosefinch. (For a more detailed list, see the introductory section of this book.)

The Pontic Alps are famous for their azaleas and rhododendron, which grow in abundance between the upper grasslands and the forests. In other respects too the flora is typically alpine, with immensely rich flower meadows on either side of the main watershed. For a detailed coverage of the flora, the reader is advised to obtain one of the specialist volumes listed in the bibliography.

History, culture and people

In Ancient Greece, the coastal strip was known as Colchis, fabled site of the Golden Fleece sought by Jason and the Argonauts. The Colchian tongue is believed to survive today in the form of the Laz language, making this the oldest language in Asia Minor still spoken.

Greek traders and settlers moved into this area, establishing various colonies, of which Trapezus (modern day Trabzon) was one of the most important. On the southern slopes of the range, the Romans colonised the steppes and valleys, establishing major forts at cities such as Bayburt. The impossibility of concerted military action in the rugged northern valleys, however, meant that this part escaped much of the Roman influence.

Later, the Turks encountered much the same situation. Rapidly colonising the dry hinterland, they were unable to make much impression on the Black Sea coastal region, which maintained its mix of Greeks, Armenians and Georgians. Trabzon itself eventually fell to the Turks in 1461, ending its period of rule as a Byzantine city state. The local inhabitants remained, however, and during the last century Russia played an important part in the region's development. Besides being the major trading partner, Russia was also official protector of the Christian subjects of the Ottoman Sultan. Evidence of this connection is still visible in the magnificent mansions around Çamlıhemşin that were built on the proceeds of trade by rich Greeks.

In 1923 the expatriation of the Greeks ended their dreams of a

43

Pontic state, and the ethnic mix of the region has remained little altered since then.

The Laz people strictly speaking occupy the coast between Pazar and Hopa, although "Laz" is often used by Turks to refer to the inhabitants of the eastern Black Sea in general. Their language, as previously mentioned, is very ancient, unwritten, and unrelated to Turkish. Characteristically blue-eyed and blond, their origins are uncertain but their language is similar to Georgian.

Further west, the valleys of Of and Çaykara speak a Greek dialect, as do the people of Tonya and Maçka. The former, however, are deeply religious whilst the latter have only a loose adherence to Islam.

The region around Çamlıhemşin is the heartland of the Hemsin folk. These people, with their own traditions, are distinct from Laz. Noticeable to the visitor is the music, with the distinctive tulum, a bagpipe often covered in blue cloth. Once heard, this sound is never to be forgotten, and conjures up images of the mists, rivers and forests of this spectacular region. Also unmistakable is the traditional women's dress of black wool skirts, patterned wool socks and orange silk headscarves. Considerably more exotic than the average Turkish dress, one could not mistake this for anywhere else.

Despite the tiny size of the Hemşin population, these people, who speak a form of Armenian, have come to dominate the Turkish pastry trade. Any Pastahanesi in any large city is likely to be owned and run by a Hemşinli.

Christian Armenians used to rule much of the Kaçkar region, but the massacres and migrations of the early years of this century mean there are virtually none left now. There are reputed to be one or two families still living around Yaylalar.

The final group worth mentioning are the Çepni communities who live in the highlands around Giresun. Adherents of the Alevi sect, they are descended from the Turkmen tribes who arrived here in the thirteenth century.

The contrast between Black Sea coast and interior is as marked culturally as geographically. From the relaxed approach to Islamic tenets found amongst the Laz to the inhabitants of Bayburt is a world away. Here, women dress head to toe in a brown "sack" which completely covers their face as well as body.

The relaxed lifestyles of the inhabitants is reflected in the festivals. Whilst festivals occur throughout Turkey, those here have a special feel to them. Any visitor here at the right time should make the effort to attend and will be richly rewarded.

The principal cause for celebration is the annual return to the yayla. It is difficult for Westerners to appreciate how central this is to the people here, but the annual migration to the uplands is invested with a spiritual quality, of retreat from the outside world and a chance to rediscover themselves.

Traditionally, the festivals begin on the first day of summer (20th May around here) and continue for three riotous days. It is now that you are likely to see the tulum produced and the traditional *horon* danced.

The most famous of all festivals, though, is the annual Kafkasör festival at Artvin. This takes place in the third weekend of June. Bulls are pitched in battle against each other, and surrounded by a large crowd of spectators. When one bull has had enough, it usually charges off through the ranks of spectators, who beat a hasty retreat. Whilst this may not be to everyone's taste, there are numerous other sideshows, from oil wrestling to folk dancers and bagpipe players.

Another noteworthy festival is the Kadırga. As big as the Kafkasör festival, this takes place on a bare mountaintop at 2100m altitude, 25km from Tonya, during the third weekend of July.

The Black Sea inhabitants have a reputation for lawlessness and picaresque, buccaneering lifestyles, stretching back at least as far as Xenophon's time. Kazantzakis' Zorba came from Crete, but would have felt equally at home in Trabzon or Rize. A case in point is the small town of Tonya, where "one half makes guns, the other half uses them". The Laz people belong to a seafaring tradition, and many are widely travelled. Others from the region make up a disproportionate number of Turkey's politicians and businessmen. Despite their success on the wider stage, these people try to return to the yayla every summer. Consequently, the person you meet in a small village is as likely to be a guest worker in Germany or a Professor from İstanbul as a farmer continuing a centuries-old lifestyle.

Access to region

The main bases for access to the Kaçkar range are the small towns of Yusufeli on the southern side, and Ayder and Çamlıhemşin on the northern side.

For Yusufeli, the nearest large city is Erzurum, which has a railway and airport. From Erzurum, several buses daily leave for Yusufeli, 128km distant, usually en route for Artvin. The bus station is located in the centre of town, not the main *otogar* on the outskirts. (Ask for Yusufeli Otogar.) First buses leave around 07.00., the journey takes 3-4hrs, and costs £2.40.

As of writing, the bus departure times from Erzurum to Yusufeli are: 07.00, 09.30, 12.30, 15.30, 16.30.

After crossing a high pass, the road descends beyond Lake Tortum into the spectacular Tortum river gorge. The main road bypasses Yusufeli, so you will be dropped at a junction 9km from the town. A taxi or minibus is usually waiting at the teahouse to take you into Yusufeli; this is sometimes included in the bus ticket price. At the start of the road up to Yusufeli is a sign which describes the town as a "fruit paradise".

To reach Çamlıhemşin and Ayder, take one of the numerous buses that ply the coastal route to the towns of Pazar or Ardeşen. From here, several buses daily run the 22km inland to Çamlıhemşin. Çamlıhemşin itself is an interesting place, being the Hemşin heartland, and surrounded by large old mansions. However, unless you are planning on visiting Verçenik, the higher town of Ayder makes a better starting point for the Kaçkar mountains. Three erratic minibuses make the journey on a road that is currently being asphalted between the two towns. The minibuses often are coming up from Pazar. Cost 60p for the 14km, 45min journey. Back down from Ayder, the buses depart 06.30, 11.00, and 13.00, and it is advisable to book beforehand at the cafe by the stream across the road from where the buses depart. If fully booked, the walk down to Çamlıhemşin takes 2-3hrs.

Bases

Yusufeli (pop. 4,000) is a lively, attractive little town at the junction of the Çoruh and Barhal rivers. There are several small hotels here, and a few excellent restaurants with terraces overhanging the river. The hotel I stayed in last time was the Hotel Barhal (tel. 9 0589 13 65), run by Sırali Aydın, located near the suspension bridge. This has been recently improved, offers rooms overlooking the river, and more importantly, the staff are familiar with trekkers' needs. Their friends (see useful contacts and addresses) have copies of the excellent 1:25,000 map.

Of the restaurants, the Mazen Fiçi Birası and the place next door are noteworthy. Saturday nights here are wild affairs, with the Tulum being produced and dancing until the small hours. There is a wide range of food shops in Yusufeli; this is the best place to stock up before the trek. Methylated spirits is available in one or two shops; stock up here as none is available in Barhal or beyond.

Yusufeli is a centre for whitewater rafting on the Çoruh river. Anyone interested should seek details in Yusufeli.

Ayder (Ilıca), formerly a large yayla, (alt. 1350m) is best known as a thermal springs resort, and often appears on maps as Kaplıca, the Turkish name for such springs. A popular place with Turkish holidaymakers, it is well supplied with hotels and restaurants. There are great plans for the future of Ayder, chiefly manifested in an enormous new bath house, quite out of keeping with the rest of the village. Ayder as a whole is an uneasy mix of traditional wooden and modern concrete buildings strewn across an alp above the fast-flowing river.

Recommended as a place to stay is the Hotel Çağlayan ("Hotel Waterfall"), several hundred metres further up from the bus halt and village centre. This is run by a young student, Kadir Sarı, who also acts as a mountain guide and speaks good English. Price £3 a night.

Also recommended, though more expensive, is the attractive wooden Hotel Saray, situated very close to the bus stop in the village centre. Rooms here cost around £8 a night. The rapid development of Ayder is pushing prices up. The restaurant Çağlayan is OK.

There are two hot baths in Ayder, at least until the new complex opens. Of these two, one is an old hamam-style affair situated across the river. Unfortunately on my last visit the suspension bridge across to it had partially collapsed. The main bath is situated down by the river, and is open to men and women on alternate days. Buy a ticket in the office just above the baths, and take your own towel. This is one of the most relaxing ways imaginable to end a trek.

Food prices in Ayder are expensive (by Turkish standards), and the choice is somewhat limited; better to stock up in Çamlıhemşin or one of the coastal towns.

Medical facilities

On the southern side of the range, the large village of Sarıgöl, midway between Barhal and Yusufeli, has a medical centre.

Starting points

On the northern side of the range, Ayder is the principal starting-point for trekking. The exception to this is when visiting the Verçenik area, in which case Çamlıhemşin is a more sensible departure point.

On the southern side, the two main starting points are the villages of Barhal and Yaylalar.

Barhal, alt. 1200m (official name Altıparmak) is a small village 32km by road upstream of Yusufeli. There are one or two basic shops, telephone, and two hotel/restaurants. The nicest of these is the one opposite the shops, with a large wooden terrace over the river. This serves beer and basic meals, including fresh local trout. Rooms are very cheap, around £2 a night. Beneath the restaurant is the village bakery.

Barhal is set at the confluence of two streams: the Barhal Çay to the NW and the Zamavan Çay to the SW. The area around the village is particularly verdant, with orchards and hay meadows amongst the hazel stands.

To reach Barhal, take one of the two daily minibuses which depart from Yusufeli. The earlier of the two departs around 14.30 and ends at Barhal, whilst the later departs around 15.30 and continues to Yaylalar. It is worth checking these times, and purchasing tickets, in advance. The journey takes 2hrs on a rough road, cost £3. En route, look out for the castle sited spectacularly on top of a rock. This is a remnant of the ancient Georgian kingdom of which this was once a part.

Yaylalar, alt. 2100m, also known as Hevek, is an attractive village of wood and stone chalets, the highest permanently inhabited village in the area. There are several basic shops, telephone, and a guest house in the process of construction. This is owned by Ismail Altınay (tel. Yaylalar 0589 4228), who used to work for Trek Travel and knows the mountains well. He can put you in touch with a local guide or arrange mule hire.

To reach Yaylalar, catch the minibus which departs daily at around 14.30-15.00 from Yusufeli. It is 24km beyond Barhal, and a further 1hr 45mins. Cost £6 from Yusufeli.

As a starting point, I would always recommend the southern, Yusufeli side of the range. Apart from the higher altitude of the roadheads, more important is the question of navigation. The omnipresent mists on the northern slopes mean that whilst you can easily follow a river downstream, it is much harder to pick the right tributary to follow in ascent.

Supplies on trek

Unlike many other mountain areas in Turkey, it is possible to obtain reasonable food supplies in the yaylas. Local cow's milk cheese, butter and *yufka* are available in most large yaylas. If fortunate, you may be able to find wholemeal bread - a nice change from the white stuff.

Maps

The best maps to the area are a series of 1:25,000 scale maps which cover the central Kaçkar range, from the Kaçkar Dağ massif in the west to Marsis in the East. These are very difficult to obtain, but Halil Meydan, c/o Hotel Barhal in Yusufeli, has photocopies of an incomplete set.

These maps form the basis for the identical maps by Bozkurt Ergor and Trek Travel. The former is available from the same source as the 1:25,000 maps, the latter from Trek Travel. For the wider range, including Verçenik, there is a small scale Turkish map, İspir-Rize B-XIII. This is difficult to obtain and lacking in detail, although it has 50 metre contours. Many of the place names bear little resemblance to those on other maps.

Guides

Several operate within the area; see Kaçkar section in Useful Addresses.

The Principal areas

These are listed from NE to SW, and this is roughly the order in which they are described in the book.

Central Kaçkar range
This consists of five main massifs or groups of peaks, all lying along the watershed running from NE to SW.
From the NE these are:

1) Marsis
2) Karataş/Altıparmak
3) Liblin Tepe
4) Bulut Dağ
5) Kaçkar

Outlying areas
Beyond this central area lie two important peaks:
   Verçenik, an isolated peak on the main watershed 40km SW of Kaçkar peak.
   Gungormez, the highest point on the ridge parallel to and S of the main watershed.

List of main peaks

(the letters after each name indicates the area in which the peak occurs; M = Marsis; A = Karataş/Altıparmak; L = Liblin Tepe/Libler Gölu; B = Bulut Dağ; K = Kaçkar; V = Verçenik)

1) Kaçkar Dağ (K) 3937m
2) Pt 3864m (K) 3864m
3) Verçenik (V) 3711m
4) Bulut Dağ (B) 3562m
5) Gungormez Dağ (K) 3536m
6) Soganlı Dağ (K) 3527m
7) Karataş (A) 3495m

8)	Liblin Tepe (L)	3472m
9)	Didvake (A)	3350m
10)	Büyük Dağ Tepe (K)	3328m
11)	Altıparmak (A)	3301m
12)	Marsis (M)	3300m

Excursions from Yusufeli

The churches of the Southern Kaçkar

The former Christian inhabitants of this region have left a rich architectural legacy in the form of several magnificent churches and cathedrals. No visitor to the area should leave without trying to see at least one of these buildings. Whilst some lie outside the Kaçkar region proper, they are all accessible from Yusufeli.

The churches were built by Georgians, up to and including the Bagratid dynasty in the eleventh century. When the Bagratids moved to present day Soviet Georgia, the architectural style they took with them greatly influenced the development of architecture in that country.

Barhal

Situated on the edge of Barhal village and near the start of many treks, this is the church most visited by tourists. It is in the form of a simple nave without transepts, of impressive size. It dates to the tenth century, being built during the reign of Magistros. Well preserved, it owes its survival to its present day usage as a mosque.

To reach the church, follow the road upstream from Barhal alongside the RH (easternmost) tributary for 10mins. The church is hidden amongst the trees up on the hillside on the right. If locked, ask for the key from one of the locals.

İşhan

One of the finest of all the Georgian churches, in a magnificent setting. 42m high and in a poor state of repair, the earliest part of the church, the apse, dates back to the seventh century. The church itself was rebuilt in the ninth century, but most of the current stonework, including the dome, dates to a restoration of 1032. There are some magnificent carved portals externally, and the dome still has some

İşhan

superb frescoes, out of reach of vandalism by Muslims. Outside, there is a baptistry in amongst the mulberry trees. To reach İşhan, take the road from Yusufeli back towards Erzurum for 44km to the Oltu/Kars turning. Follow this road for a further 7km, to where a side road (signposted İşhan) heads up L steeply for 6km to İşhan. There is a small cafe in the village.

Dörtkilise

As the name suggests, there were originally four churches here, but only one survives. Somewhat confusingly, the old (Georgian?) name is Otkhta Eklesia, translating as "eight churches". Situated high in an isolated tributary valley of the Çoruh river, this church is still fairly intact. Although clearly neglected, the Turkish government are apparently about to provide funds for its restoration. In style the church is similar to the one at Barhal, being a single massive rectangle, tall and narrow in proportion. Like Barhal, it was built under the reign of Magistros.

To reach Dörtkilise, take the İspir road out of Yusufeli (unmetalled). Follow this above the Çoruh river as far as the village of Tekkale, 7km distant.

On leaving Yusufeli, there is a ruined building visible on an island in the river, where it curves right. This is a watchtower, which lines up with one at Tekkale, situated on top of the large, fortified plug of rock which dominates the village. By this means, people in and around the churches at Dörtkilise could be warned of approaching trouble, the watchtower at Tekkale being visible to them.

At Tekkale there is a "Resting Place", run by Cemil Aybarak, a pleasant man who offers basic food, drink and accommodation here. Immediately past the "Resting Place" is a sharp R turn, in the village centre, which leads up a very rough, barely motorable road for a further 7km to Dörtkilise.

Osk Vank

Another church built during Magistros' reign, this enormous building is now abandoned. The church has a dome which has partly collapsed. There are a few frescoes still surviving, giving a hint of what the place must have been like in its heyday.

The Çoruh valley, just W of Yusufeli

To reach Osk Vank (Oshki) head back towards Erzurum. At the southern end of Lake Tortum, a dirt road, signposted to the church, leads in 7km to the village of Çamlıyamaç and the church.

Khakhuli

In its prime, this was the most celebrated of the monasteries in the area, and is fortunately in a reasonable state of preservation today. It consists of a main basilica, very beautiful, and several smaller chapels. The triptych from here, in gold and enamel, is still to be seen on display in Tbilisi, and is widely regarded as the greatest work of medieval Georgian art.

To reach Khakhuli (Haho), head towards Erzurum. 15km S of lake Tortum, an unmarked dirt road heads W, to Bagbasi village, where the church complex is located. (NB. this is shown as Chacho on the 1:800,000 Lascelles Eastern Turkey map, and as being close to the village of Dikmen.)

Karataş/Altıparmak area

The term Altıparmak (lit. "six fingers") is, like much Turkish nomenclature, loosely used. There is the peak of that name (3301m) overlooking Karagöl. An alternative usage is for the whole range of mountains from Karataş in the West to Marsis in the East. The third occurrence is as a name for the pinnacled ridge which extends NE from Altıparmak peak towards the Marsis group.

To keep matters simple, in this text any references to Altıparmak refer to Altıparmak peak, unless qualified as "Altıparmak ridge". I will avoid using Altıparmak as a term for the wider mountain group.

The best campsite is by the beautiful mountain lake of Karagöl, alt. 2650m. The starting point to reach this is Barhal.

K1 Karagöl from Barhal

From Barhal, take the right fork in the village just beyond the mosque (ie. don't cross the bridge as for Yaylalar). NB. The peak visible on the road up to and beyond Barhal village is **Didvake 3350m.**

Follow the motorable track alongside the Barhal river, passing two recently constructed lodges after 30mins. At a yayla reached after 50mins, the road follows the river round to the L, then crosses a ford and continues on the RH side to where the road starts to switchback. (Alternatively, at the ford, continue on the L bank for 30m to a wooden bridge and concreted spring to rejoin the main track.)

At the first switchback, take a path which crosses the scree to follow an irrigation ditch, and up through terraces to regain the road in 10mins or so. There are fine views of Altıparmak peak and the Altıparmak ridge from here.

Almost immediately, leave the road again for an easier path next to the river on the RH bank, passing under a small overhang on a hewn-out track. Switch banks to follow a delightful path through conifers, with a yayla on the opposite bank. Ahead (W) is an obvious broad grassy ridge with two yaylas superimposed on its crest. Aim

55

for this ridge and follow the path alongside the drainage channel which runs down from the yayla.

The two yaylas of Naznara (below) and Amaneskit (above, 3hrs from Barhal) are idyllic in high summer. Apple orchards surround the houses, some of which have their own small trout ponds. There are numerous beehives on the porches to complete the image of self-sufficiency.

I found the people here some of the most hospitable in the Kaçkar range, and on my first visit spent several hours helping collect wild redcurrants, which were being pressed to produce juice - very welcome on such a hot day.

Rising in tiers above the upper part of Amaneskit are several tiny water mills, used to mill rye and dried beans. Bone dry inside, I was offered the use of one instead of a tent during a storm. Unfortunately, they were only suitable for those under 5ft 6ins.

It is possible, and well worthwhile, to buy wholemeal bread and local cheese here. Being made from cow's milk, it is reminiscent of Swiss cheese, and makes a nice change from the ubiquitous *beyaz peynir*.

From the highest of the buildings in Amaneskit (3hrs from Barhal), follow the path steeply up the broad grassy ridge, alongside a watercourse, for 15mins (still heading W). The path then takes the LH side of the ridge, and in a further 5mins reach trees and an easing of the angle.

Skirt the trees on their L, and continue along the crest in a SW direction. 10mins from the first trees, take a horizontal path on the R which leads into a cwm with waterfalls, then zigzags up L over scree to gain an aqueduct (4hrs from Barhal). Follow this watercourse for 100m or so before gaining a track up L through scree and dwarf rhododendron (10mins).

For the next section, you are basically aiming for the scree slopes to the L of the crags with a waterfall angling down through them. The path is easily lost hereabouts, but it tracks back R above the crags to reach Karagöl quite abruptly (4³/₄-5hrs from Barhal).

Excursions from Karagöl

K2 Altıparmak 3301m

A fine peak which is perfectly feasible for a half day; the keen can climb this in a day from Barhal if camping at Karagöl. Fairly straightforward for the most part, the actual summit ridge involves some awkward (II/III) scrambling. In early season, steep snow may be encountered gaining this ridge.

From Karagöl, the peak appears to be a simple cone. Aim straight up from the lake in a NNW direction, over scree and rock, to gain the skyline. This proves to be a subsidiary spur running eastwards, and it gives fine views of the Marsis group in particular. The best views, however, are given to those who persevere as far as the main summit.

Cross from the spur (steep snow likely) to gain the ridge, which soon becomes a spectacular knife-edge, leading to the summit rocks in 200m. The summit cairn is now visible. One short difficult step of 5m (II/III) is best taken on the right (a cairn is visible as a route marker). $2^{1}/_{2}$-3hrs to summit from Karagöl.

The summit has a register (take a pen!); I found that a friend of my father's, Brian Spenceley, had climbed this peak with a Leeds Polytechnic expedition in 1976. My ascent on 12th July was the first that year: a combination of heavy winter snow and very few visitors. As this is quite likely to be the first Kaçkar summit many visit, it is worth describing the view in some detail.

The Altıparmak ridge nearby to the NE looks quite reasonable from this viewpoint. N is the deep valley containing Dere yaylası. The fine peak between and behind Pt 3270m and Marsis is Pt 3406m. Didvake is the bounding ridge above Karagöl to the SW/WSW, whilst behind Didvake to the right is Karataş (3495m), one of the most impressive peaks in the Kaçkar range.

Looking along the main range SW, the big peaks are: Liblin Tepe (3472m); Bulut Dağ (3562m); and Kaçkar Dağ itself (3937m). Beyond in the far distance are Germaniman (3434m) and Verçenik (3711m), the shapely cone, which has a slightly Matterhorn-like appearance from this aspect.

The cwm behind Karagöl - Didvake on L. Photo taken late July

Descent: either retrace your steps, or, just as easy and more interesting, continue some way back down the summit rocks then down an easy rock gully SW to gain the the broad snow-filled cwm leading easily to Karagöl. There is a good chance of seeing Caspian snowcock in the cwm.

An interesting diversion is to head up to the obvious gap at the head of the cwm. This affords a view down into the northern valleys. On the other side of the col is a short scree slope, followed by a steep 40ft snow couloir, which eases off in angle to reach a lake (often frozen).

K3 Didvake 3350m

The ridge which is visible on the walk up from Barhal, and even on the approach from Yusufeli, gives another rewarding day out. The summit crest gets progressively more difficult, with exposed scrambling and culminating in a hard (grade III) section to gain the summit pyramid. Worthwhile even if the final difficult section is omitted. Seen from Karagöl, Didvake dominates the head of the cwm and presents a seemingly impregnable line of huge cliffs. The route described makes an exhilarating traverse along the skyline above these cliffs.

From Karagöl, head W up into the cwm, then take the LH branch up to the col between Nebisatgur (3050m, the lower ridge on the L) and Didvake. Ahead, there is an obvious large gendarme on the main ridge, which looks impassable, and a gap to its R. In fact, either way is feasible, the former avoiding the steep snow which can linger in the couloir leading up to the gap.

From the col, head SW up a rock and scree rib, trending leftwards, then either head up L to the very foot of the rock gendarme, or swing back R (W) to follow the couloir or rocks on its side to reach the main ridge crest. The gendarme is passed easily by following a rake which heads diagonally leftwards below its face, then skirts round the back to rejoin the second alternative at the head of the gap.

Looking across (W) from the main ridge, Karataş is now seen in its entirety, very close at hand on the opposite side of the snow basin. Keep your eyes open for chamois in this basin. The Liblin Tepe massif is also seen well from here.

Didvake from the slopes of Altıparmak

Follow the superb ridge, running roughly SE-NW, on well bedded-down blocks. (Moves of I/II depending on how closely the actual ridge crest is followed.) Descend carefully to the deep notch before the summit pyramid. Climb a chimney/crack for 8m (crux, III), then easier ground to the pinnacle top. A fantastic, extremely narrow crest (II) leads to the final summit block. $2^{1}/_{2}$-3 hours from Karagöl.

Allow nearly as long on the descent to the col; if conditions permit, enjoy the 400m (vertical height) glissade down into the cwm!

K4 Nebisatgur 3050m

The attractive ridge forming the southern side of the Karagöl area. It is a pleasant ridge walk-cum-scramble (grade I) with none of the "big mountain" feel of its larger neighbours. It can be done comfortably in an afternoon, and affords the easiest means of viewing the main Kackar peaks from Karagöl area.

By far the best way is to traverse Nebisatgur; the route described goes from W to E; go the other way and you may reap the rewards of the glissade previously mentioned.

Head W up into the cwm, then take the LH branch up to the col between Nebisatgur and Didvake (as for the previous route).

Continue along the ridge to the summit of Nebisatgur (1hr 45mins from Karagöl). The continuation ridge leads without difficulty back down to Karagöl.

K5 Altıparmak ridge c.3150-3200m

SWmost point

Fairly straightforward, but a long approach, being best tackled from the north. From Goltegi (see Altıparmak from N description), head up ESE to the gap between the Altıparmak ridge and Altıparmak peak. From here, easy scrambling leads directly up to the summit. There is a final short, difficult section, with moves of II/III to gain the summit block. (It may well be possible to find a way which avoids this section.) 3hrs from Goltegi.

Onward routes from Karagöl

Unless you cross the col at the head of the cwm to gain the N side of the range, the only real onward route is over to the Kışla valley, which is the next valley south.

K6 Karagöl to Piskenkaya/Kışla valley

Both above and below the watercourse beyond the trees, 40mins or so below Karagöl, numerous tracks contour the hillside. There is not a lot to choose between them, they all lead round into the upper Kışla valley and end up at one or other of the yaylas below Piskenkaya. The lowest track, which heads off just above the tree-line ridge, gives the easiest ground but loses slightly more height by emerging lower down the Kışla valley. Allow 3-4 hours.

K7 Alternative route via Nebisatgur/Didvake col

Worth the trip if you haven't already been as far as the col, this also offers a quicker way of reaching Piskenkaya.

Gain the col between Nebisatgur and Didvake (1hr). From here, head pretty much straight down the valley, tracks after a while appear. Follow these on the RH (west) bank, and continue dropping down until you enter the main Kışla valley. It is possible to drop down to the main path up the valley by the river, but it makes more sense to follow tracks round the hillside which join up with this just below Piskenkaya. 3hrs 30mins from Karagöl.

K8 Approach to Altıparmak/Marsis area from N

This approach would make an interesting alternative to the usual route from Barhal. I have walked the upper sections around Goltegi and Antor yayla, but haven't come up from the coast. However, this appears to be the correct way from the map. Anyone trying this approach should ensure that they are in the Tunça Deresı (valley); once there, it is hard to go wrong.

From Ardeşen, take a minibus to Aşağı Durak. Shortly before there, a track crosses a tributary on the L and continues to Eski Armutluk. This is in the Tunça Deresı. Following this upstream will lead you past Çalimlı Yayla, and continuing in an ESE direction you pass Neknali Yurdu and Movri Yayla. Shortly beyond Movri Yayla, the valley forks, with one branch heading due S, the other branch heading E, before forking again quite shortly.

To reach Altıparmak and the SW end of the Altıparmak ridge, take the S branch, with a track on the E side of the river, to reach Dere yayla at 2000m altitude (45mins from valley fork). From here, continue S up the valley for another hour to reach a tiny, primitive yayla by a lake, known as Goltegi. This is the best base for tackling the southern end of the Altıparmak ridge. Continuing up the valley, in a SSW direction, skirting the lake on its W shore, leads to the large higher lake of Samlı Gölu in 20mins. This is another beautiful campsite, and is a good base for ascents of Didvake from the N.

To reach the Marsis area, continue up the E fork of the Tunça Deresı to reach the next fork shortly. Here, take the southernmost fork, which heads in a ESE direction, with a track on its N side, to reach Magara Yurdu after an hour or so, and the higher yayla of Antor, 2350m, in a further few minutes.

At this point, the valley kinks sharply to the L, and leads up to Hevek Gölu. This is at the northern end of the Kaçkar proper, and is not further described.

From Antor, head directly up the hillside opposite, in a ESE direction, to gain the ridge, c.2850m, in 1hr 30mins from Antor, between the two peaks of Antor Başı 3169m to the S and Pt 3201m to the N.

Directly below you is one of the lakes, c.2700m, which encircle the head of the Gudadashor Deresı. Either camp here and explore the area, or contour round S to reach the collection of small lakes which make the best base for investigating the Marsis area (see next section).

Marsis and associated peaks

This area lies at the northern extremity of the main Kaçkar range, and is very little visited by walkers. Whilst not as high as other major peaks, these mountains nonetheless have considerable charm. Several high mountain lakes set in the midst of the cirque of peaks provide an ideal base from which to explore.

Amaneskit yayla with Altıparmak behind, Altıparmak ridge on right

Approaches

K9 From Barhal

Follow the route as for Karagöl to reach the yayla of Amaneskit. You are now aiming eventually for the defile which separates Pt 3270m from Marsis (3300m), roughly N of here. From the highest houses here, a path contours R round the hillside. This soon steepens as it begins to parallel the stream. Keep going up (ie. not along the irrigation ditch), which soon eases off after 15mins, to pass through low conifers heading in a W direction. Cross a water channel, then cross a water channel again. From here, descend to cross the main stream at a couple of rickety wooden planks (35mins from Amaneskit).

Up the opposite bank, ascend gently on a faint grassy track, which leads to a faint traversing path heading N. Take this through bushes, then conifers, on a ridge above a collection of half a dozen houses (55mins). (NB. This point can also be reached by cutting across the main valley at a point before the ridge up to Naznara and Amaneskit; probably a bit quicker.)

Take the lower RH fork at a junction; the LH fork leads to the same place but is rather overgrown.

Take the well worn path which heads diagonally L to the river. Steeply up, crossing the watercourse, to gain a track heading back L on a slight ridge into the cwm proper (2hrs from Amaneskit). There are one or two reasonably flat campsites near big boulders in the cwm bed, or a nice walled-in enclosure on the R just before arrival.

The very impressive crags of Pt 3270m lie due N of here. Heading N, skirt to the L of a cascade via a snowpatch and slabs to the R of a large black boulder, to a flat section below another 20m high rock step (2hrs 25mins). Bypass this on the R, then back L, climbing easy-angled slabs just to the R of the stream. Attain a position just below the foot of Pt 3270m (3hrs). Skirting these crags, the cwm leads on in a NE direction to a snow basin between Pt 3270m and Marsis.

The summit of the pass is reached by following the snow bowl. On the other side of the col, another large snow bowl leads down into the fine corrie mentioned in the introduction.

The Altıparmak ridge, Pt 3270m and Marsis (far r) from the summit of Altıparmak. The peak between Pt 3270 and Marsis is un-named, 3406m.

The Altıparmak ridge as seen from Naznara

Mt Ararat (photo: J.Newton)
The mountains behind İşak Paşa Saray, Doğubeyazit

There is a choice of camping spots by the lakes - the first one is reached just a few hundred metres beyond the end of the snow bowl by a small lake.

K10 Approach from Sarıgöl

The outflow from these lakes leads down into a deep valley, the Gudadashor Deresı, with several yaylas, which eventually joins the main Barhal river near Sarıgöl. I haven't walked this valley, but route-finding should cause no problems if you choose this as a way out from here.

Approach from NW
As for previous section on approach to Altıparmak, route K8.

K11 Approach from NE

Whilst it is possible to reach the Marsis range from Artvin, it makes more sense to start from the town of Borçka. Catch a minibus to Göktaş and on to Kabaça. Following the road, then track, up this valley will lead you to the NE side of the Karataş/Marsis peaks. (NB. this Karataş is not to be confused with the larger peak of the same name in the Altıparmak area.)

K12 Marsis 3300m from col (between Marsis and Pt 3270m), Grade III

An attractive mountain, well seen when approaching from Naznara and Amaneskit. According to local legend, this is another contender for resting place of the Ark.

I ascended Marsis in typical Kaçkar weather - thick mist and drizzle. In common with many other summits in the range, this consists of a series of tops separated by clefts. It is quite possible, therefore, that there exists an easier way to gain the main summit than the one described.

From the head of the snow bowl, it is possible to ascend scree to gain the summit crags of Marsis, joining them at a notch between the main summit and a subsidiary summit to its L (NE).

This notch is very narrow, and contains a prominent wedged boulder. Climb the sharp crested ridge which leads directly from

Pt 3270m, Marsis, and Pt 3332m from the summit of Altıparmak

here up to the summit block. This is the hardest (Grade III) section, and is even harder when the rocks are at all greasy. Allow 2hrs from the col/head of snow bowl.

K13 Marsis 3300m from Naznara side, Grade III

It is possible to ascend Marsis directly from here, to gain the notch between the two summits as described in the previous route. The absence of any decent campsite until halfway up to the col by Pt 3270m, however, reduces the attractiveness of this route.

For those who wish to try this way, attain a position just below the foot of Pt 3270m on the L. Head SE over broken ground to reach a small ridge crest. Gain what appears to be a faint path, heading just N of E up the LH side of the broad scree ridge crest. Continue in this line to reach the foot of the summit crags (1hr 30mins from Amaneskit).

These are best passed by continuing up the ridge just L of centre for a few metres, then tracking back diagonally R, which turns into a shallow gully. Traverse R easily below the top of the gully to gain a broader scree shoot coming down from the R. Keep to the R, spiral round to the R (E), and back to the notch with wedged boulder (2hrs). Follow the previous route to the summit.

K14 Pt 3270m

From the cwm which leads to this peak and Marsis (when approaching from Amaneskit/Karagöl), a snow gully is visible on the peak's S side. Attain this gully, and follow it, 40ft, and take the LH branch near the top. The summit is further back than expected; the impressive face on the R is merely the termination of a spur. 2hrs from cwm bed to summit.

K15 Altıparmak ridge - NE top (also see route K5)

To the L of the snow gully mentioned on the previous route, a broad, easy snow gully leads up to the main watershed ridge at a col. From the col, it is a simple walk up to the summit. 2hrs from cwm bed.

Liblin Tepe area

The main peak in this central area is Liblin Tepe 3472m, although it also makes the best base for attempting Karataş 3495m. The high lake of Libler Gölu, 2750m, is an ideal camping spot. The principal yayla below Libler Gölu is Piskenkaya.

K16 Approach from Barhal

The quickest route involves following a rough tractor track alongside the Kışla river as far as Piskenkaya yayla. This is pleasant but not as scenic as the route up to Karagöl. If you want to feel the turf beneath your feet and are not pushed for time, take one of the routes described that cross the ridge from Karagöl area to the upper reaches of the Kışla valley.

From Barhal, cross the river and follow the road in the direction of Yaylalar for 45mins to where a steep-sided tributary valley comes in from the W. This is the valley that leads up to Piskenkaya and is the next tributary S from Barhal. Follow the road on the RH side, at a junction just by an electric pole and bridge. (There is a beautiful late season campsite in the hay meadow by the river, just below some wooden barns.)

After 30mins cross a concrete bridge. There is an old path on the RH side leading up to a small attractive yayla (don't take this). 1hr from the junction, encounter fields and barns as the valley starts to curve slightly to the W. Fine peaks soon come into view due W, the main one being Liblin Tepe. After 3hrs from Barhal, just S of W ahead, can be seen an obvious col on the skyline - this is the Kırmızı Gedik which leads over to Avusor.

Continuing, you soon pass the small yayla of Kurdat. Cross a ford, beyond which the road becomes immediately disused. Follow this up to where it ends, then cross the river to the L bank and follow a good track eventually to cross the river again and reach the yayla of Piskenkaya. Alternatively, instead of crossing the river, head up R to a collection of barns, then along a track to Piskenkaya (4hrs from Barhal). There is a chance of seeing red squirrels in the forest just below Piskenkaya.

To reach Libler Gölu from here, continue up the valley through the village, to cross the river (second bridge you pass), and follow its L bank uphill, heading due W. Where the main river curves away to the S, aim ahead for an obvious waterfall through a gap. Ascend the slope on the L of the waterfall (some bushwhacking through low scrub) to emerge at Libler Gölu, an attractive setting. $2^{1}/_{2}$-3hrs from Piskenkaya.

K17 Liblin Tepe 3472m from S (Libler Gölu)

A large, isolated massif with twin summits, of which the Easternmost point is slightly higher. A substantial part of this route is on easy angled snow, making it very pleasant underfoot, in contrast to the other high Kaçkar peaks.

From Libler Gölu, cross the valley northwards and up to a subsidiary ridge. Follow a tongue of scree to gain another subsidiary ridge, from where a long rising traverse R gains one of the slender gullies (snow in early season) which lead up into the big south-facing snow basin. Alternatively, this basin can be gained by scrambling up the rock band to the L of the gullies.

Easily up the snow basin towards the gap between the two summits. Before reaching this, avoid the large gendarme by scrambling to the R, to reach easy angled scree which leads up to the highest summit (3hrs 30mins from Libler Gölu).

Follow the same line in descent.

Liblin Tepe 3472m from East (Demirkapı Gölu)

Seen from the Karataş/Didvake peaks, Liblin Tepe appears possible from this direction, at a similar standard to the normal route, though with greater route-finding skill needed. I can't confirm this, however.

K18 Karataş 3495m

Alongside Verçenik, this must surely rank as one of the finest of the Kaçkar peaks. A slender rock pyramid, it is not easily seen, being hidden behind Didvake when approaching from the Barhal side. It has two summits separated by a narrow col from which a snow couloir descends on the E face. The westernmost summit is the higher of the two.

My attempt to climb Karataş was via the steep central couloir, well seen from Didvake (see photo opposite page 32). I reached the col between the two summits, but thick mist and lack of determination caused me to turn back.

Seen from Bulut Dağ and Liblin Tepe, however, the mountain presents a gentler aspect. With the aid of binoculars I was able to scout out a reasonable looking line up the S face. This is the line described. I'd be interested to hear from anyone following my directions who can confirm this. Naturally, I avoid describing routes I haven't done, but Karatas is such a magnificent peak that several readers may be willing to give it a go.

From the yayla of Norsel, just downstream of Piskenkaya, a tributary comes in from the N. Follow this up to Sultan Yaylası, where there is another branching of the stream. Take the RH branch, the Ipilçeda Deresı, which heads up just W of N into the cwm between Karataş and Didvake. Rather than continuing up to the head of this, skirt the SSE spur of Karataş by heading NW. From here, it looks as though a scree/snow slope of gentle angle leads directly up to the summit block.

Onward routes

There are three main possibilities:

1) via the Kırmızı Gedik to Avusor and Ayder
2) via Oküz Gölu to Körahmet and Yaylalar
3) to Karagöl and the Altıparmaks (as described in reverse from Karagöl, routes K6, K7).

K19 Piskenkaya to Avusor and Ayder

From Piskenkaya follow the Onbolat Deresı to Libler Gölu as previously described.

The Kırmızı Gedik is the obvious high pass ahead. Due to its height (3050m), the pass is little used and the path is very faint. The trick is just to head W, aiming for the RH side of the col. This is steep going, but the col is reached in 1hr 10mins from Libler Gölu. The summit of the pass is a surprisingly broad grass bank, with snow patches lingering until late summer. Those tackling the pass early

The col of the Kırmızı Gedik, looking towards un-named peaks east of Bulut Dağ

in the season may encounter some steep snow below the top. There is a good view of Kemerli Kaçkar and of the myriad rock peaks around Bulut Dağ from the col.

In descent, a path runs diagonally off R before switching back into the centre of the snow funnel. Run steeply down this, all very exhilarating, to gain a flat meadow with a meandering stream and a few stone shelter remains. This is often snow-covered. Keep to the R of the stream, which soon drops over an edge. Rather than following the steepening edge of the stream, keep well to the R on a faint path through boulders.

This leads, intermittent at first, down to grassy tracks and on to the yayla of Avusor. In mist, just keep the river 100m or so to your L.

Avusor is a bare, stone-built yayla seemingly full of children. Either rest here for a while if invited in for tea, or continue downstream to pass the yaylas of Dobaya and Taşlık.

The path enters conifers, then hazel stands, all the while losing height gradually. If in mist, generally keep low; there is a path which contours out onto a long spur, and is best avoided.

The track eventually becomes motorable. Follow this down to where there is a hairpin bend 100m above the river. Ahead, the road ends suddenly. Take the hairpin down to the river, where there is (at the time of writing) a recently-collapsed bridge. This is easy to cross, however, and leads to a continuation logging road on the opposite bank.

Follow the logging road, which is in a bad state of repair, seemingly for ever. It contours round a spur, then drops back down, heading upstream, to join the main road between Ayder and the upper Kavron valley. Turn L (downstream) and follow this road down to Ayder. 6hrs from Libler Gölü, 8-9hrs from Piskenkaya.

K20 Piskenkaya to Oküz Gölü and Körahmet

This delightful walk, as well as having some fine mountain scenery, has the added attraction of staying on the drier eastern side of the range. Thus, it is suitable for days when the main ridge is shrouded in mist.

Just beyond Piskenkaya Yayla a stream drops down from a hanging valley on the L (S). Gain the path, which climbs steeply at first, into the hanging valley. Continuing in a generally SSW direction, you reach Bulut yayla, at 2750m one of the highest in the Kaçkar. It consists of a few low stone shelters, and was deserted in mid-July when I went past (2hrs 30mins from Piskenkaya).

From here, follow the stream up, just S of W, to reach a high grassy basin which contains the small lake of Oküz Gölü. This is an attractive camping spot, and it may well be worth aiming to reach here in a day from Barhal.

From the lake, climb SW to cross the ridge. If time permits, Pt 3305m, E along the ridge from this col can be climbed easily from here (1½-2hrs round trip).

Descend from the ridge to gain a path which leads down to Körahmet yayla, passing near the two upstream yaylas. Either descend to one of these if continuing to the Körahmet Geçidi, or carry on downstream to Körahmet yayla and Yaylalar village.

Walking towards Adatepe yayla in the Körahmet Valley. Part of Bulut Dağ in the background

The Körahmet Valley and Bulut Dağları

This is the deep valley north of Yaylalar, containing one of the most interesting of the Kaçkar peaks.

K21 Approach to upper Körahmet valley

The entrance to the Körahmet valley is unmistakable - 500m downstream from Yaylalar, an old packhorse bridge is next to a new concrete bridge on the N side of the Hevek river.

To gain the Körahmet valley from Yaylalar, cross either bridge and take the road following the tributary upstream. This forks after 100m - take the higher fork. It becomes a well-made track which contours the hillside 100m or so above the river. Even in late July, the river hereabouts was bridged by 20ft thick snow.

Delightful walking along this track leads to the first yayla of Adatepe. By this stage, the Bulut Dağları dominate the view ahead. En route to this yayla, I spotted a flock of brilliant pink rose finches at around 2300m.

In the yayla itself there is a lovely old drinking fountain with an Arabic inscription and date. It is hard to believe that Adatepe is only inhabited for a few months each summer, the buildings look so substantial.

Continue to pass another yayla shortly (the existing maps seem to credit this valley with more yaylas than occur on the ground). The buildings here are also substantial, and this is Körahmet Yaylası. Beyond here, though, the valley becomes more U-shaped and the final yayla of low stone shelters is attained shortly before the valley forks.

At the fork, the LH branch heads SW. At its head lies the fine looking rock peak of Çaymakçur Tepe (3420m), and hidden out of sight to the R is the major Körahmet pass.

The shorter RH branch leads NNW up into a cwm and a possible route over to Avusor or Libler Gölü (see onward route K26 for details of both).

Bulut Dağları

The name means "misty mountains", and it is well deserved.

Collectively forming the headwall of the Körahmet valley, there are two main summits at either end of an inclined ridge running roughly NNE-SSW. The lower, southern point is Pt 3224m, whilst the more substantial northern neighbour is Bulut Dağ (3562m). Just north of Pt 3224m on the ridge is a high (c.3100m) col which leads over to Palakçur and eventually Ayder (not to be confused with the better known Körahmet pass slightly further S).

It is worth explaining some of the confusion that occurs on existing maps. Bulut Dağ is sometimes erroneously referred to as "Kemerlikaya". This is clearly a reference to Kemerli Kaçkar (3125m), an isolated peak just NW of here.

The best campsite and starting point for an ascent of these two peaks is at the confluence of the two main streams, where the valley forks, a few hundred metres beyond the highest yayla.

K22 Ascent of Bulut Dağ 3562m (avoidable grade III sections)

This magnificent route, covering some impressive terrain, takes the skyline ridge running from L to R up to the summit.

From the campsite, in between the two main branches of the valley lies a cwm, roughly WNW of here. A faint zigzag path leads up the LH side of the stream that issues from the cwm. An hour's walking leads up into the cwm and a possible campsite by some boulders.

From this point, take the RH side of the cwm to gain a snow tongue. Up the side of this, into a higher cwm. Head up this to gain the skyline ridge at a small col immediately R of a conspicuous gendarme (2hrs 45mins total). Alternatively, and somewhat easier though longer, aim well to the L of the gendarme to reach the main ridge near the prominent large col. The col is in fact a double one, and either side leads down to the yaylas of Palakçur now visible below. Pass the gendarme easily on its W side to regain the previous route at the ridge crest.

Move round onto the SW face, keeping high, and cross a small cwm to a ridge on the far side (it is possible to gain this point directly from Palakçur via a long scree slog). Much of the going is over loose scree - this is one of those routes which could be much easier in early season under a decent snowpack.

By this stage, you should be about 100m below the main ridge crest. There are a few useful meltwater springs here. Gaining the top of this subsidiary ridge is tricky. Either a) cross a steep (45ft) snow slope, b) climb 10m of steep grade II/III rock, or c) descend much lower and climb back up scree on the other side of the ridge.

Climb the ridge on excellent granite (III), keeping to its L side, or again avoid difficulties by a scree slog to the L, to reach a subsidiary summit (4hrs).

Continue easily along the ridge crest to the summit in another 15mins (4-4$^{1}/_{2}$hrs total from campsite).

The summit is graced by a wooden tripod and a small stone windbreak. The main Kaçkar watershed elbows back R towards the Altıparmak peaks here, ensuring a particularly good view from the summit. All the main peaks are visible. Büyük Göl and Avusor are below to the NW.

In descent, take the same route.

K23 Pt 3224m

This is an easy ascent from the Körahmet pass; it could readily be taken in on the way over to Çaymakçur. Seen from the Körahmet valley, Pt 3224m is unmistakable - a narrow snow ribbon descends the full height of the peak from the summit in a straight line.

From the campsite follow the LH branch of the main valley along a reasonable grassy track, a bit indistinct at times, until the obvious weakness in the W-bounding valley wall that marks the Körahmet Geçidi (pass) becomes apparent. Head up to the pass and gain the col without difficulty (1hr 45mins). Weather permitting, you can see the upper reaches of the Cennavit valley and Cennavit Gölu below you.

From the col, where sacks can be left, take the ridge which leads up, generally NNE, to the summit. Avoid rock steps on the ridge crest via detours onto the L (W) face, and gain the summit in 1hr from the col.

In descent, the easiest option is to retrace your steps as far as the Körahmet geçidi. Alternatively, if returning to the campsite, descend the NNE ridge to the col between Pt 3224m and Bulut Dağ, and so back to camp. This is more interesting and quicker than retracing your steps.

There is a third alternative.... the snow gully descending from the summit offers a 2000ft glissade for the adventurous. Certainly the quickest way off the mountain, but check from below that all the snow is there first!

Onward routes from the Körahmet valley

There are four main possibilities:

1) Via the Körahmet geçidi to Yukarı and Aşağı Çaymakçur.
2) Via the pass between Bulut Dağ and Pt 3224m to Palakçur.
3) Over the Lale geçidi to Avusor (ice axe and crampons advisable).
4) Crossing the col between Büyük Taş Tepe and Pt 3305m to Oküz Gölu and Piskenkaya (ie. as previously described in reverse from Piskenkaya, route K20).

Also, there is a minor variation from the head of the valley over into the Düpedüz Deresı.

K24 Via the Körahmet geçidi to Yukarı Çaymakçur and Ayder

One of the easiest means of crossing the Kaçkar range, but none the less enjoyable. It could be done in a long day from Yaylalar.

Follow route K23 as far as the Körahmet geçidi (1hr 45mins). Descend, passing near Cennavit Gölu, to follow a track on the R side of the Cennavit river. This is crossed after approx 45mins from the col, and the hillside is contoured round to gain another tributary valley and the yayla of Yukarı (upper) Çaymakçur. (It is possible to continue alongside the river and miss out Yukarı Çaymakçur.)

Follow the track from here down through Aşağı (lower) Çaymakçur yayla eventually to join the Kavron valley at the motorable track leading down into Ayder. Allow 6hrs to reach Ayder from Körahmet.

K25 Via Palakçur to Ayder

Follow route K22 as for the ascent of Bulut Dağ as far as the double col on the main watershed. (2$^{1}/_{2}$-3hrs). The RH col provides a marginally easier descent. Drop down scree and snow slopes without any difficulty to gain the Palakçur valley and yayla. A good path leads from here down to join the previous route shortly before the Kavron valley.

K26 Via the Lale Geçidi to Avusor and Ayder

The pass lies at the head of the right-hand (NW) branch of the Korahmet valley, and is the most difficult way of crossing the main range from here. Certainly in early season this involves steep snow - an ice axe and preferably crampons are prerequisites. I actually missed the pass proper when I came over this way, but I have seen both sides of the correct route. If this does not put you off, then the reward is some spectacular cliff scenery en route.

From the campsite, it is probably best to follow the river upstream, heading NNW. Alternatively, retrace your steps as far as the highest yayla, to gain a track which leads back up the hillside in a NW direction to emerge on a less steep slope overlooking the RH valley branch. (Don't take any northerly tracks, as these lead up to the pass over to Oküz Gölu.)

By keeping on the R flank of the valley and avoiding snow, you emerge into a broad cwm, with a prominent needle of rock bisecting a snow col on the skyline ahead. This impressive feature marks the Lale Geçidi. The cwm itself is a pleasant spot, with a small lake and several stone shelters dotted around. It would make a good, though cold, camping spot.

My mistake from this point was to continue up the valley, which curves round to the R. After gaining the ridge ahead, an unpleasant scramble led down a gully to a snow slope overlooking Libler Gölu. From here it was a fairly straightforward matter to traverse across leftwards to the Kırmızı Gedik and so down to Avusor. This is best avoided. From the Lale Geçidi, however, it appears to be a long, smooth snow slope down into the cwm E of Kemerli Kaçkar and on to Avusor.

In mist, the path down to Avusor keeps the river fairly close on your LH side.

Avusor is the first yayla you reach, and it consists of a series of low stone buildings, in contrast to some of the more substantial yaylas hereabouts. Continue downstream to Dobaye Yaylası. Beyond here, numerous paths skirt the hillside; if in doubt, take the major or lower path. Eventually, after passing another yayla, the path becomes a track, which ends quite abruptly at a bend in the road. Follow the logging road down L to the river and a collapsed bridge - it is possible to cross on temporary planks. Exciting stuff above a raging torrent! Keep on this logging road, which skirts round a spur and heads back upstream to join the main road down to Ayder from the Kavron valley. Take this, passing a large collection of beehives en route.

K27 S to Dobe and the Düpedüz Deresı

Whilst not a major route, this variation has the benefit of being a quick way from the head of the Körahmet valley to Dobe without losing height. As with the route via Oküz Gölu to south bounding ridge between Kazankaya (3187m) to the W and Kargeke tepe (3060m) to the E.

Head S along the stream emerging from Şeytan Gölu, at its confluence with the stream that comes down from the Körahmet Geçidi. This kinks round to the R (W) and Şeytan Gölu. Continue in

Kemerlı Kaçkar on the right, as seen from the top of the Kırmızı Gedik

the easiest line steeply up to gain the ridge crest, and a steep grassy descent down to Dobe Yaylasi. (This route misses out Şeytan Gölu, but it is a pleasant spot and worth the slight detour. Also camping possibilities.)

K28 Kemerlı Kaçkar 3125m

This detached peak is overshadowed by its near neighbours, but is a worthwhile ascent. The best approach is from a campsite on the high meadow at the foot of the northern side of the Kırmızı Gedik.

From here, head S into the cwm between Kemerlı Kaçkar and Bulut Dağ, until a prominent snow ribbon (40ft, ice axe needed) gives access to the summit cone (see photo). The summit itself is gained via an easy scramble. 2-2$^{1}/_{2}$hrs from campsite.

Kaçkar Dağ area

Containing the highest peak and some of the most attractive high valleys, this area is a popular one with visiting trekkers.

K29 Approach from Yaylalar

From the village of Yaylalar, head up a side valley to the S, taking the road round above the village to get back into the main valley. Pass some lovely wooden houses and barns, but as yet no real views of mountain peaks. You can buy strong local cheese here, as well as hand-knitted thick socks (a curious mixture of merchandise!).

Continue through idyllic flower meadows to the small hamlet of Olgunlar, 2100m, 1hr.

There is a fine old house here, together with a small wooden verandah overhanging the stream. This was built by a man who had worked in Germany, and who decided that something was needed to welcome foreign visitors to the village. It is a touching, idiosyncratic monument to the hospitality of everyone throughout this region.

Continue up the broad valley, marvellous walking, for a further hour to reach the much more primitive yayla of Nazaf. All along the banks of the Büyük Çay are dippers, and small flocks of red-fronted serin.

Continue up the valley, passing beneath the towering cliffs of Kaçkar Dağ and its near neighbours. A dramatic deep valley between Kaçkar Dağ on the L and Mezovit 3760m comes into view, characterised by a huge recent rockfall in its lower section. This valley leads up to a 3305m pass between the two peaks. This would be an exciting journey, and looks difficult; I have no further details.

The main valley steepens and narrows just beyond this side valley; continue up to reach a broad, flat meadow known as Dilberdüzü. 4hrs 30mins from Yaylalar. In reverse, allow 3hrs from here back to Yaylalar.

The meadow is used as a permanent camp throughout the summer season by Trek Travel. There is a walled-off section of stream for bathing, and the site is generally very attractive, with enough room for several parties. If a group is in residence and you prefer solitude, the alternative is to carry on to Deniz Gölu or one of the other lakes near there (see Normal Route description, K31).

K30 Approach from N - Kavron Valley

Primarily used by mountaineers tackling the serious N face of Kaçkar Dağ, this approach can also be used by anyone starting from Ayder wishing to climb the normal route.

From Ayder, take the main road upstream out of the town, and follow this, taking the RH fork at the junction with the road in from Palakçur and Çaymakçur (ie. keep to the main valley on the R(W)). It is often possible to hitch a lift over this section early in the morning.

The Kavron valley is a dead straight, deep smooth valley running N-S. Follow the road as far as the lower of the two settlements in the valley, Aşağı Kavron. From here, the path continues upstream, crossing the river to its W bank, to reach Yukarı (upper) Kavron.

The head of the valley is encircled by the various spires and outliers of Kaçkar Dağ. The usual starting point for ascents of Kaçkar Dağ itself is the meadow by Oküz Göl, altitude 2970m. To reach this from Yukarı Kavron, continue due S upstream for some considerable way until you encounter the next large tributary which comes in from the L (E). This is the Mezovit Deresı, and leads steeply up to the high pasture around Oküz Göl. Immediately in front of you is the impressive N face of Kaçkar Dağ, and the fine spire of Kaçkar Tepe. Sidney Nowill, in his *Alpine Journal* article (see bibliography), regards this as one of the finest campsites anywhere. Interestingly, he mentions a stone wall across the mouth of the rocky stream 300m below here. This is the bull wall, placed here to keep the bulls separate from the cows for the duration of the summer. 2hrs 30mins from Yukarı Kavron, 6hrs from Ayder.

To reach the southern side of the watershed from the Kavron valley, instead of turning off to Oküz Göl, continue due S up the main Kavron valley, following the stream bed on its E side. Attain Derebaşı Gölu (nice camping spot). 3hrs 30mins from Yukari Kavron.

From Derebaşı Gölu, the track heads SW up to gain the crest of a ridge, which separates the Kavron valley from the Polovit valley. Follow this ridge in essence, but drop down slightly on its W side to pick up a path which heads SSE to the Davanali pass c.3150m. If you can't find the track in the lush grass, simply keep near the ridge crest. 1hr 30mins from Derebaşı Gölu.

Drop down into the Davali deresı from the pass, then skirt round at a fairly high level, across several intervening spurs, below Pt 3864m. This leads round to Soğanlı Göl (3hrs from Derebası Gölu), from where a short hike N over the small col leaves you at Deniz Gölu and the normal route up Kaçkar Dağ. It is probably better to camp at Soğanlı Göl: there is greater availability of flat ground here.

Kaçkar Dağ 3932m

The highest point in the range, and a substantial massif with numerous outlying peaks. It is here that the few remaining glaciers lie. Its height and relative ease of access and ascent mean that Kaçkar Dağ is also the most popular mountain hereabouts. A must for any visiting party.

K31 Normal route via S face

An easy ascent over rock and scree with no technical difficulty.

From Dilberdüzü, follow the stream uphill, on a grassy path, towards the valley head (roughly SW in direction).

Up and right is a large scree and boulder slope which leads up into a deep cwm to the L of Kaçkar Dağ proper; the route essentially aims for the LH side of this cwm. Toil up this slope to reach the finely-situated lake of Deniz Gölu (2hrs from Dilberdüzü).

This attractive spot makes a fine campsite, and there are onward routes from here over the col immediately behind the lake. There is space for two to three tents. Depending on where you are heading to next, this can be preferable to camping at the busier Dilberdüzü.

From Deniz Gölu, skirt round the lake and gain a broad snow tongue which leads up a valley. Follow this to its head, drop down and traverse rightwards over mixed scree and snow patches (faint trail in places) towards the rockband which lies below the easier-angled summit scree slopes. Drop down into the head of a large valley, and skirt round this to gain slabby ground leading to the obvious passage through the water-streaked crags which guard the summit slopes. Through this to the easy-angled scree bowl. 3hrs 45mins.

Above, the path takes the obvious easiest angled ground, first R for 200m, then L, then back R just below the left bounding ridge. It is a further hour from the rock band to the summit. $4^{3}/_{4}$-5hrs from Dilberdüzü.

The summit itself is on a fine crenellated ridge, and there is a summit register in amongst the rocks. As you would expect, the view from Kaçkar Dağ is the most extensive of the Kaçkar peaks, with the whole of the range being visible, and beyond to the Caucasus on a clear day. Mount Ararat is reputed to be visible also, but I can't confirm this from my ascents.

Descent: retrace your steps, allowing $1^{3}/_{4}$-$2^{1}/_{4}$hrs down to Deniz Gölü, and a further 1-$1^{1}/_{4}$hrs back to Dilberdüzü.

K32 Variation via Dar Boğaz Grade I/II

An easy scramble, with one awkward step, through the impressive deep slit in the cliff opposite the campsite, affording a quicker and more interesting way up Kaçkar Dağ, particularly when combined with descending via the normal route. In early season, the gully may be blocked with snow, although this should be obvious from below.

From Dilberdüzü take the much narrower RH of the two scree gullies which split the face. Head for 30mins up the scree, entering the confines of the Dar Boğaz (lit. "narrow pass"). There is a short step of grade I/II.

Above this, emerge onto a remarkable flat meadow, very lush and with a small lake. (This would make a magnificent campsite were it not for the impracticalities of carrying full kit up the gully.) Head W up a grassy rake, NOT over R to the big stream. Keep in this general line, passing numerous patches of brilliant primulus, to reach two tiny lakes together.

Now head WNW/NW, to the L of a prominent rock buttress (1hr), to emerge in a big valley running across the summit slopes of Kaçkar Dağ; the normal route crosses this valley higher up. There is another small lake to your L. (The RH side of the rock buttress overlooks the lower part of this valley, and is a possible route, but involves some descent.)

Avoid losing height by skirting several small cwms on the L.

Start to cross the valley before you reach the large moraine/scree mound, and aim across slabby ground to the obvious passage through the crags which guard the summit slopes. Through this to the easy-angled scree bowl, and regain the normal route. 2hrs 45mins.

Above, the path takes the obvious easiest angled ground, first R for 200m, then L, then back R just below the left bounding ridge. It is a further hour from the rock band to the summit. 4hrs total from Dilberdüzü.

K33 Pt 3864m

The second highest point in the Kaçkar, and a very impressive bit of rock, it rises above the glacier at the head of the Deniz Gölu cwm. There don't appear to be any easy routes up it, and I know of no further details.

The cwm continues round towards Kaçkar Dağ with several steep rock pyramids forming the bounding wall.

K34 Soğanlı Dağ 3527m

This small peak lies SW of Dilber Düzü, and offers a short, pleasant walk with good views.

From Dilberdüzü, head SSE to the Hevek pass, gaining a faint but definite track through the moraine. This steepens and becomes trackless, but leads to a well-defined exit on the RH side of the pass. 1hr 15mins. NB. Don't take the well-defined track to the col over on your L a few hundred metres away. There is a good view of Pt 3864m from here.

From the col, it is an easy 45min scramble to the summit of Soğanlı Dag, which offers fine views SW and of the long, featureless Devali valley.

From the summit, a small lake, Soğanlı Göl, is visible to the N, with a good campsite by it. The low, narrow scree col immediately behind it drops directly into Deniz Gölu, passed on the ascent of

Kaçkar Dağ. It is 30mins to Soğanlı Göl, or keep high on the ridge to gain the normal path between the two lakes. Allow 45mins from the summit to reach the edge of Deniz Gölu, and a further 15mins to skirt it by scrambling. Take care in early season, as there can be steeply banked snow running into the lake.

K35 Büyük Dağ Tepe 3328m

Another short walk, this is the mitre-shaped peak lying due E of Dilberdüzü. Follow the previous route towards the Hevek pass, but take the well-defined track to the E. This leads up onto the summit ridge, from where the top is easily gained.

Onward routes

K36 To Ayder via Çaymakçur Geçidi

This route follows the exquisite Düpedüz valley, over the Çaymakçur Geçidi (pass) and down to the yayla of the same name. It is one of the most attractive, and easiest, ways of crossing the range.

From Yaylalar, walk to Olgunlar, 1hr. You are now aiming for the subsidiary valley which heads up to the NW. Go up through the village, keeping on the R bank of the subsidiary stream. After 10mins, keep on the higher path, not the one down to the river.

The main route from Olgunlar skirts the hillside above the village, and is steep to start. The route described is more direct and attractive.

After 35mins, the valley makes a sharp curve round to the L, and heads W. It was at this point that I had one of my scarier moments whilst trekking. I emerged round a corner to find a large bull snorting and pawing the ground a few metres in front of me. I headed diagonally away from it, through the fields, and fortunately it decided not to follow.

45mins out from Olgunlar, pass a small, primitive yayla, which is normally deserted until the end of July. NB. From here, a path traverses diagonally up the steep hillside on the L (S). This leads over to near Nazaf Yayla, and as such represents a quicker way from Çaymakçur pass to Dilberdüzü than descending to Olgunlar.

Ahead, the valley opens out to assume a broad glaciated form.

After approx. 2hrs 30mins, the path starts to head up the RH valley side (indistinct) towards the hidden Çaymakçur pass. This section of the walk is exceptionally beautiful, passing through masses of wildflowers. The valley head is delineated by a series of jagged rock spires, unclimbed as far as I know. You will quite probably lose the path hereabouts, but the direction is obvious - towards the deep side valley that is the Çaymakçur Geçidi. Head due W.

Once in the side valley proper, there is a track in the rocky bed. If you lose the path, head in a NW direction along the bed of the valley. There is an abrupt finish to gain the top of the pass, where a small side valley drops into the cwm. Continue NW to reach the top. 4-4$^1/_2$hrs from Yaylalar.

Still heading NW, descend on a good, well-defined track towards Kara Deniz Gölu. There are several lakes scattered around the northern slopes of this pass; it is very easy to lose them in mist. If the weather is fine, Kara Deniz Gölu or its neighbours Meterel and Büyük Deniz Gölu offer fine campsites.

The path peters out after 35mins on a broad grassy ridge - keep on the L side (still NW). Kara Deniz Gölu is somewhere over to the L. If you miss it, head N from the broad grassy ridge, and continue N to overlook a N-flowing valley and a yayla on the opposite bank. This is the Çaymakçur valley and the yayla of Yukarı (upper) Çaymakçur.

Head steeply down to the yayla, and cross by a wooden footbridge at the top of the village. 1hr 30mins from pass. Continue along a track which is part-paved with large granite flags, to the top end of another yayla, positioned in a narrow "V" to avoid avalanches. Keep on the RH bank, and drop down through rhododendron, then forest, to reach a good track which eventually merges with the road from Kavron coming in from the L.

From here, it is a long trudge down to Ayder on the road previously described in the Körahmet pass and Libler Gölu/Avusor routes. 4hrs to Ayder from Çaymakçur pass, 8-8$^1/_2$hrs total from Yaylalar. A long day, which you may want to break with a camp en route.

K36A Variation: Çaymakçur Gecidı (pass) to Upper Kavron valley

From the top of the Çaymakçur pass, descend as far as Kara Deniz Gölu. A faint track heads due W for a short while, over a ridge, then drops down to follow the Çinaçur Deresı to emerge just downstream of Yukarı Kavron.

K37 Continuing W

From Dilberdüzü, it is possible to skirt the heads of the valleys on either side of the main watershed and eventually reach the Verçenik area. I have been part way from each end, but have not done the whole traverse. Such a trip would take in much of the best the region has to offer.

Once again, for ease of navigation, the southern side of the watershed is preferred.

K38 Trek to Dokümacılar and the Çoruh river

This fine walk crosses the ridge to the south of the main Kaçkar range. It has the attractions of better weather and of being little visited.

From Yaylalar, walk to Olgunlar (1hr). From the lower end of the yayla, a tributary stream descends from the Sern side of the valley. The path basically follows this. Cross the main Hevek river and gain a path (faint at times) alongside the tributary. This leads roughly S up into a cwm between two spurs, keeping nearer to the westernmost spur.

The path then starts to track slightly eastwards towards a col on the ridge. Attain this col, c.3000m. 2hrs 30mins from Olgunlar; $3^1/2$-4hrs from Yaylalar.

The col is situated between the two peaks of Beytepe 3175m to the W, and Kanuçar Tepe 3173m to the E.

Either of these peaks is an easy ascent from the col. From either peak it is possible to continue along a ridge giving a magnificent panorama of the main Kaçkar range. Heading SW from Beytepe, the ridge passes Pt 3333m, then in another 1.5km attains the summit of Binsirt Tepe, at 3408m as high as many of the main range peaks.

If time permits, leaving your sacks at the col and heading along the ridge for a section is highly recommended.

Descend in a generally SE direction from the col to reach the headwaters of the Kara Kekik ("black thyme") river. Follow this down on its NE bank to enter the Hüngemek Deresı. The path leads to Yukarı Hüngemek, c.2000m altitude. Just beyond Yukarı Hüngemek, there is a fork in the track; either continue steeply down to cross the river and reach Aşağı (lower) Hüngemek, or continue contouring, round the ridge, to gain the Peterek Deresı and the village of Peterek. Either route leads down into the main Çoruh valley, several km upstream of Tekkale village.

K39 Gungormez Dağ 3536m

The highest peak outside the main Kaçkar range, this shapely mountain is well seen when looking south from many of the Kaçkar summits.

There are several possible means of ascent. From the col near Beytepe, it is possible more or less to follow the ridge eastwards, over Kanuçar Tepe and Şarkınet Tepe, to reach Devside Tepe 3358m. This in turn leads over Pt 3519m to the summit of Gungormez Dağ. Although there are no real technical difficulties apparent, this would mean spending a lot of time above 3000m, necessitating a bivouac.

Alternatively, and more directly, it appears that the ridge to the W of Devside Tepe can be reached from the yayla of Modut Yurdu.

From Kaşbaş (Mikelis), a village on the road before Yaylalar, follow the Mikelis river S, then follow a tributary WSW to gain Modut Yurdu, 2400m. From here, it appears possible to gain the main ridge SW. There is a large lake, Kartal Gölu, at 2900m below the cwm head.

I haven't tried either means of ascent, but there doesn't appear any technical difficulty on either route.

K40 Samisdal

This fine walk is one of great contrasts, from rhododendron forest to alpine meadow and rocky ridge top. It can be done as a round trip from Ayder, or as a variation approach to the upper Kavron or Polovit valleys.

NOTE: *This route crosses the river on a suspension footbridge. On my last visit to Ayder (1992), this had partly collapsed and was impassable. Unless it has been repaired or replaced, the following notes are redundant!*

From below the hot pools, cross the footbridge and pass the old hammam on the opposite bank. Take the narrow trail which goes horizontally at first, past a fallen tree, then begins a muddy climb.

Continue upwards on an overgrown, but clear, path alongside attractive waterfalls. It may be hard to believe, but this path is well-used by locals. The vegetated nature is merely a result of the fertile soil and climate.

After 45mins, emerge at a clearing by a waterfall. Cross the stream here and continue up the opposite side.

After 1hr 20mins, there are fine views SW to a yayla on a ridge, with a mountain behind. Reach a faint junction in a further 25mins and take the lower, better defined track. Descend to the river (in quite a large valley) and cross via a log bridge. 2hrs 15mins. On the ridge above you is the yayla of Hazındak. Zigzag up through trees and meadow to gain the Hazındak ridge, where there is a large track and spring. 2hrs 45mins.

The yayla, composed of substantial single-storey huts, was deserted at the end of July, and is an extremely attractive place - to my mind one of the most beautiful of all the Kaçkar yaylas.

Head up through the village and gain the ridge ahead, which trends SE. There is a good view S to Karadağ (3214m) and the perfectly U-shaped Polovit valley, with Polovit yayla at its bottom RH toe.

Keep along the crest for several hundred metres, then the path tracks along the R side of the ridge. There are several woodpeckers in this area.

Follow this magnificent track, which continues traversing the steep hillside, to round a corner and have a view up the valley. 3hrs 10mins. The big yayla 1km ahead in the bottom of the valley is Polovit. (The high track on the hillside above Polovit leads over to Tirevit.)

Keep on the path, which leads up to Samisdal yayla, built of granite blocks and situated in a rather bleak hollow. 4hrs 30mins from Ayder.

(A classic viewpoint for the N face of Kaçkar Dağ is Memişefendi Tepe, 3066m, a short distance due S of Samisdal. Allow 45mins to the summit.)

A high track leaves Samisdal in a SW direction to Apıvanak. The route now described, however, aims for the Kavron valley.

Continue E up the cwm, and after 10mins, start to ascend the L bank, where the valley turns R. (In mist, maintain a course due E.) Don't be misled by the good track heading up R.

It is 15mins to a slight ridge, and continue E up a steep bouldery slope, then slightly S of E, move across the slope, to gain a ridge. 30mins from Samisdal.

This ridge runs N-S, and at its lowest point, towards the S, there is a well-defined track descending diagonally R down the hillside. It soon turns S to Yukarı (upper) Kavron, so don't take this unless you want to go that far up the valley. Instead, head straight down the steep grassy hillside, heading slightly N of E, to hit a nearly horizontal track after 10mins L along this, it soon switches back through knee-high rhododendron. The path is intermittent - if you lose it, keep going straight down. I descended this hillside in very thick mist - there may be a proper descent path, but I was unable to find it. What is certain is that you can't go far wrong by just descending as directly as possible.

Keep on the R of a big gully near the bottom. It is 1hr from Samisdal to reach the river in the Kavron valley bottom, opposite and below the yayla of Aşağı (lower) Kavron. At this point it is necessary to wade the ice-cold river - good fun, but care required. There is usually someone fishing for trout on this stretch, who will no doubt give you a hand crossing if you ask. 1hr 30mins to yayla from Samisdal.

From here it is 40mins back down the road to the junction with the road from Çaymakçur, and on to Ayder in a further hour. $7^1/_2$-8hrs round trip.

Verçenik area

Introduction

This area, at the southwesternmost end of the Kaçkar range, feels detached from the main peaks due to the distance separating the two areas. In fact, there is a continuous ridge linking it to Kaçkar Dağ, but this is overshadowed by the dominant peak of Verçenik itself.

This mountain is, to my mind at least, the finest in the whole of the Kaçkar range. It is also technically the most difficult. Add to this the remoteness of the area, interesting approaches, an almost total absence of visitors, and a collection of other fine rock peaks, and it all adds up to something rather special - even by the standards of the Kaçkar.

K41 Approach from N - Çamlıhemşin

From Çamlıhemşin, catch a minibus to Varoş (preferable) or Çat. 2hrs 30mins, £2. These tend to leave early to mid-afternoon.

The road runs alongside the roaring Fırtına Çay, and passes through some very interesting country. Hay meadows cling to the steep slopes, and up in the mists are some magnificent old mansions. These date back to the last century, and are of remarkable size and elegance. They mainly belonged to rich Greek traders who had made their fortune in Russia.

Further architectural splendours occur in the form of slender packhorse bridges, of which there are several en route. They are similar in design to those found on the southern slopes of the range, though somewhat larger and more elegant. Some of these have been dated to the seventeenth century; others are probably older.

An hour or so out of Çamlıhemşin is one of the most memorable sights in the region - the ruined castle of Zilkale. Perched on top of a crag, covered in ivy and moss, it lies in a Caspar David Friedrich landscape of forests, mountains and swirling mists. Its origins are obscure, as are the reasons why anyone would wish to build a castle in such a backwater. Explanations vary, from a sixth-century origin in the Lazic wars of Justinian, to it being built by Genoese in the

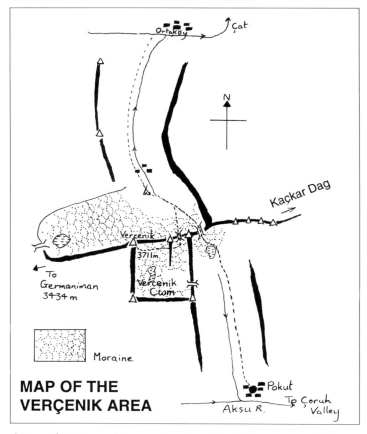

MAP OF THE VERÇENIK AREA

thirteenth century. It seems implausible that anyone could have conceived of a trade route through here, however.

From Zilkale the road continues steeply up, getting progressively worse, to reach a small bridge which is crossed to Çat, a short way up the opposite bank. If you are in a bus going to Varoş, stay on board. Otherwise, get off here and continue on foot for 5km up the road (ie. don't cross the bridge) to a similar bridge at the turn-off to

Varoş, 1km distant on the opposite bank.

The chances are it is rather late by the time you arrive at this point. There is a decent camping spot 45mins up the road (still on W side of river) where a ramp cuts back up to a grassy platform. The alternative to this would be to stay at the small Hotel Cancık in Çat.

The road leads pleasantly up through the conifers to the yayla of Ortaköy, above the treeline (2hrs 30mins). Opposite the campsite is a large yayla, known as Kale. The ruins of Varoşkale are meant to be visible somewhere near, but thick mist has prevented me ever seeing them. Perhaps you will be luckier.

Ortaköy is a large yayla in three separate sections. From Ortaköy, a long, flat bottomed valley runs S. Verçenik lies at the head of this valley, but is not yet visible.

A minibus departs Ortaköy at 08.00, so presumably it is possible to reach here by bus also - however, I have yet to find one! The road along which you have travelled, incidentally, continues past Ortaköy in a westerly direction, skirting the foot of Balikligölu Tepe (3352m), before dropping down to Incesu and one of the Hemsin valleys.

Head up the valley from Ortaköy, taking the cow track in preference to the road, to see Verçenik come into view after 45mins. Another 15mins leads to a primitive stone yayla, above which there is a very pleasant camping spot on a flat meadow beside the stream. This is probably the most comfortable base for ascents of Verçenik.

K42 Approach from S - Çoruh valley

Due to the lack of minibuses frequenting the upper Çoruh valley, it makes more sense to start from the town of İspir, rather than Yusufeli. There is at the time of writing no public transport between the two towns along the Çoruh river. İspir is a pleasant little town, from where it is possible to stock up on essentials.

From İspir take a minibus alongside the Çoruh river to the very large village of Aksu Köyu, 17km downstream. In case you have a bus which is carrying on down the valley, look out for a large modern bridge crossing the river, with a small PTT on the opposite bank. Get out here, and cross the bridge. Aksu Köyu is a couple of km up the road on the R.

From Aksu Köyu try to pick up transport to the village of Pokut;

if this is not possible, take a bus or lift going to Çatakkaya. Either will take you further up the Aksu valley to where it forks. Çatakkaya is straight on; Pokut is further up the valley to the L. Walking from this junction, it should take around 1hr 15mins to reach Pokut.

Pokut is a very attractive wooden and stone village perched on a ridge 100m above the road. It has an upper and lower part, and is inhabited all year round. There is an extremely basic Bakkaliye, and the locals here were some of the most friendly I have encountered on my travels in Turkey. Coming down from a long day on Verçenik, we were given a truly magnificent meal on platters brought out from several houses. It had apparently become a matter of honour amongst the inhabitants as to who should feed us. Sitting talking to the people here on a warm summer's evening, with a scops owl sounding in the distance, was one of the most memorable episodes of my time in the Kaçkar. When I asked them if they had many foreign visitors, they mentioned a French group who had passed through about fifteen years ago.

Pokut is easy to recognise when approaching from downstream - look for the distinctive two level village, surrounded by poplars. Get off just by a wooden bridge over a tributary, and head up to the village via a steep path on the L.

The tributary valley of which Pokut is on the E side leads up to the pass between Verçenik and the Tatos peaks. It is easy to find the path from Pokut, which climbs up on the E side of the valley. I have described this in reverse, coming over from Ortaköy and the N side of the range.

K43 Verçenik 3711m from Ortaköy campsite Grade III/IV

A magnificent day out, taking a route which spirals its way around the mountain, providing views in all directions.

Looking northwards from the campsite, immediately L of Verçenik is a very prominent rock spire. The route goes between this and Verçenik.

Head up into the large basin below Verçenik, taking the easiest line (40mins), then up SE towards the notch. The going is heavy on this stretch, stepping over unconsolidated boulders.

From the edge of the scree bowl (chamois sometimes visible

here) go ESE to an easy col, then a further 20mins leads to a cairned col.

Traverse across scree in a SE direction for 300m, then straight up a slight weakness to attain an impressive brèche, with views of the slabs which lead up to the summit of Verçenik.

Continue in the same line (ie. on the northern side of the mountain), keeping close to the rock wall, to reach the main brèche above a steep snow couloir.

Descend L (S) down scree and skirt round to the centre of the face (3hrs from campsite). Some difficulty may be encountered in crossing steep snow to attain the rocks - an ice axe could be useful here. It is possible to leave axes and excess gear at this point.

The real difficulties start from here. Easy (grade I/II) scrambling trending L leads to a notch in the S ridge (3hrs 40mins). This provides a splendid view of the peaks W of Verçenik, principal of which is Germaniman 3434m.

Continue up the E side of the S ridge, and cross to the L of a large cave. Keeping low, traverse above the cave to a difficult step (III/IV), which constitutes the technical crux of the ascent. Continue from here up slabs, choosing the easiest line, to reach the summit. $4^1/_2$-5hrs total. Views are as you would expect from an isolated high peak - extensive. The line along the ridge passing Hunut Dag to Kaçkar Dağ can be made out from here.

In descent, take the same line, taking care to negotiate the difficult traverse above the cave at the correct level.

Other Peaks in the area

K44 Germaniman 3434m

This attractive, isolated peak lies well to the W of Verçenik, and is a terminal point on a spur N of the main watershed.

I have never climbed the mountain, nor do I know of any ascents, but doubtless it has been ascended by several Turkish climbers. It could provide an interesting challenge to the adventurous.

From the S, the most sensible approach would appear to be to continue up the main valley beyond Pokut, trending NW, then steeply up to gain the valley rim. From here Germaniman lies just E of N, and (probably) reachable along a curving ridge. If this mountain is like others in the Kaçkar range, there may well be an easy means of ascent from this side.

Verçenik cwm

As previously mentioned, the cwm S of Verçenik is bounded by some fine peaks. Looking from Verçenik, these are:

Kahnut Dağ 3431m

The left-hand (easternmost) of the two peaks which form the southern wall of the Verçenik cwm. Less impressive than its near neighbour, it is nonetheless a worthwhile objective.

Un-named peak c.3450m

W of Kahnut Dağ, this mountain has an impressive N face when seen from Verçenik.

A visitor to this area could do a lot worse than camping in the Verçenik cwm for a few days and climbing these mountains. If approaching the area from the S, it would seem sensible to ascend Verçenik directly from the cwm, avoiding the circuitous approach from the north.

The Tatos Dağları c.3450m

When walking over the col from Ortaköy to Pokut and the southern side of the range, these are the granite towers along the ridge towards the main Kaçkar range . A traverse of the tops is likely to be a super "Cuillin Ridge", shorter but sharper.

K45 Onwards to Pokut and the Çoruh valley

From the campsite, head SE over rough ground (no discernible path) to reach a cairned col between Verçenik and Tatos Dağları, taking the LH side of the big rock buttress. 2-2¼hrs.

From the col, which affords fine views back over the Black Sea valleys, descend E to a lake (45mins from col), on snow, and meadow and nice campsite. This is much easier going than on the

Lake Van area. On the slopes of Sulpan Dağ. Aygır Gölu and Van
Golu in the distance
The Çilo mountains from Yüksekova

Emli valley, with Kaldı (r) and Gürtepe (l)
Looking towards Sokullupıŋar and the entrance to the Narpuz gorge

N side!

250m below is a broad glacial valley running NNW-SSE. On the opposite side of this valley is a steep diagonal track. Skirt round the lake (10mins), then go steeply down the RH side for 30mins to reach the good track on the opposite side of the river. (In ascent, look for the next big recess on the L after the recess with the good track leading into it.)

Pass the entrance to the Verçenik cwm on the opposite side of the valley. There is a good view of the peaks encircling the cwm from here.

Keep on the LH (E) side of the valley - don't cross the bridge, this leads to a yayla round the corner. Towards the bottom the valley curves slightly as it joins the main Aksu valley. The path turns briefly into a small watercourse - ahead are fields and the road down to the Çoruh valley. Up on the R, on the opposite bank, is a small yayla with substantial houses. Almost immediately on the L the large Yayla of Pokut comes into view. This is reached easily in 10mins. (3hrs from col, $5^{1}/_{2}$-6hrs from N side of Verçenik.) A marvellous day's walking.

West of the Kaçkar

Beyond the Kaçkar proper, the main ridge of the Pontic Alps continues westward for 200km. Whilst the peaks may not be as impressive or high, the valleys and high alps retain a similar aspect. In this area it is possible to walk for days through yaylas of wooden chalets, flower meadows and past glacial lakes, all the while covering ground that has virtually never seen a tourist. As a place to experience yayla life, and to get a feel for the Black Sea mountains, it has much to offer.

One place worth a visit is the beautiful lake of Üzüngöl. More often than not shrouded in mist, this romantic spot is 46km inland from Of, itself 25km W of Rize.

Further west still are several ruined monasteries hidden in the hills. The much-photographed Sumela is the most famous of these, but also worth visiting are the following: Peristera (known locally as Hizir Ilyas Manastiri) lies near the village of Simsırli, 15km from Esiröğlü, N of Trabzon, situated on top of a rocky hill, in an impressive location. Vaselon monastery, 6km by rough road from the small village of Kiremitli, 14km upstream of Maçka on the main road, has some remarkable frescoes, though horribly vandalised. These monasteries, abandoned in the early part of this century, have an air of great melancholy about them, added to by the omnipresent mists.

Recommended Itineraries.

It is hard to recommend a poor itinerary in this marvellous area - nominating a particular valley or peak omits an equally attractive neighbour. If the weather is fine, then try to spend some time on the northern slopes. The ultimate trip would be a traverse of the whole range from Verçenik to Marsis and beyond, possibly continuing to Artvin. Climbing peaks along the way, this would take in all the major areas, and need two to three weeks.

A traverse of the range can be done in numerous different ways. Starting from Barhal, to Karagöl, then via Piskenkaya, Oküz Gölu and the Körahmet Geçidi to Çaymakçur and Ayder is one possibility. This would take around five days excluding peaks.

Alternatively, if you wish to climb Kaçkar Dağ: starting from Yaylalar, via Dilberdüzü, Kaçkar Dağ summit, Deniz Gölu, Soğanlı Göl, over the Davanali pass to the Kavron valley and Ayder, possibly via Samisdal. A short trek, this needs three to four days.

Then there is the route south to Dokümacılar, the traverse of the Verçenik area... the list is endless.

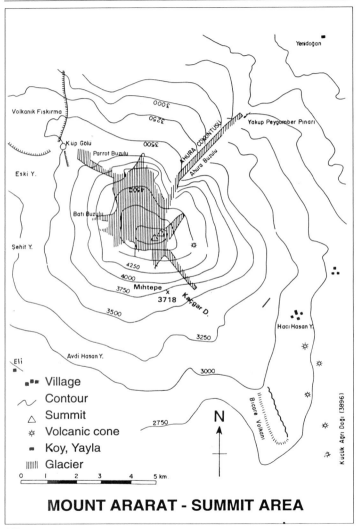

MOUNT ARARAT - SUMMIT AREA

Village
Contour
Summit
Volcanic cone
Koy, Yayla
Glacier

0 1 2 3 4 5 km.

PART FOUR

Mount Ararat

In the heart of Greater Armenia is a very high mountain, on which Noah's Ark is said to have rested. It is so broad and long that it takes more than two days to go round it. On the summit the snow lies so deep all the year round that no one can ever climb it. But on the lower slopes... the herbage is so lush and luxuriant that in summer all the beasts from near and far resort here... and yet the supply never fails.

Marco Polo, AD c.1295

Introduction

One of the best-known mountains in Asia, the highest point in Turkey, and famous in biblical legend, Mount Ararat (5137m) needs little introduction. A broad, snow-capped volcanic cone, it lies near the border with Iran and Armenia (former Soviet Union).

Its claim to fame is as the supposed resting place of Noah's Ark after the flood. Josephus writing in AD70 gives a second-hand account stating that the remains were both visible and accessible. Rather like the Loch Ness monster, "sightings" of the Ark occur with just sufficient regularity to sustain this belief. A piece of wood found a few years ago near the summit caused great excitement; this has subsequently been dismissed as being part of the base of a theodolite set up by Russians last century. Ararat, incidentally, is not the only mountain within the boundary of ancient Armenia to be credited with this honour.

Originally part of the Urartian kingdom centred around Van, the name "Ararat" is believed to be a corruption of "Urartu", although the etymology is by no means certain. Their successors, the Armenians, persisted in this area and have reputedly left several churches on the northern slopes, sadly inaccessible today. There was even a fair sized town, Ahora, which thrived in medieval times.

At present, the mountain is home to the Kurds, whose numerous yaylas dot the seemingly inhospitable slopes. Summit meltwater and springs allow rich pasture to grow in amongst the obsidian boulders - a fact alluded to by Marco Polo.

This region of Turkey lies on a major fault line, and in addition to periodic earthquakes there are more spectacular events. One such was the most recent eruption of Ararat on 2nd June 1840. This buried the abandoned town of Ahora under lava. Numerous other substantial lava flows are visible on Ararat's flanks, particularly just west of Eli village.

Permits and associated bureaucracy

Given its history and stature, it is not surprising that Ararat is a popular goal for climbers. Unfortunately for the prospective suitor Ararat lies in a politically very sensitive area. The Turkish border here is one of the very few points where a NATO country abuts directly onto a part of the former Soviet Union. Consequently, the Turkish authorities have been reluctant to allow people to wander here at will. With the break-up of the Soviet Union and decline in East-West tension, it remains to be seen whether this will lead to a relaxation of present restrictions. For the time being, however, these remain in force and it is important that you are aware of them.

Foremost is the requirement to have a **trekking permit**. These are obtainable from the Turkish Embassy (see useful addresses section), and there are two sorts: "Sportive" and "Research". Unless you genuinely want to look for the Ark, the former is the one you need. Be warned - this can take up to three months! In any event, allow three months if applying from home. The Embassy writes to Turkey, and waits for a reply before finally issuing a permit. The bureaucracy is literally Byzantine.

It is advisable to write to the embassy with name, date of birth, passport details etc. to receive even an application form, which will ask for the same information, together with your planned itinerary. Phone calls seem to have little effect.

It is quite possible to apply for a permit whilst in Turkey, and at least you will not have to worry about international post delays. Contact the Ministry of Tourism and Culture (see addresses). The waiting time is still six weeks, which should put most people off. If you are in Turkey, don't have a permit, and really want to climb

Ararat, the best bet is to approach one of the organised trekking companies such as Trek Travel. (Chances are, you will be climbing the mountain with such a company.) They are used to dealing with the bureaucracy, but even they reckon to need a month. Sometimes they can get a permit for you in less time, but it would be foolish to bank on it.

Organising the trek

Once you have obtained a permit, unfortunately the rules do not stop there. An official guide is required, and strictly speaking this guide is not meant to let you out of his sight whilst on the mountain. Add to this the transport, mule hire, provisions, tents and so forth, it is hardly surprising that the vast majority of climbers travel with one of the trekking companies. Quite honestly, you may as well pay the extra and travel with them. Much as I value independence, there are times when going it alone is just too much hassle.

For those who have ignored the last two sentences, here is how you go about organising your own trek:

1) Find an **authorised** guide. Anyone else is useless. The authorised guides are TDF certified, and you can usually find one in season (the climbing season, that is!) hanging around the main hotels in Dogubeyazit. Expect to pay £25 a day for his services, and you need to hire the guide 5 days minimum.

2) The guide needs to carry a radio transmitter/receiver; he will hire one and charge you for it. £30 for the trip.

3) Transport to Eli/Cevirme village; hire a minibus for £20.

You may want to come to some arrangement for collection after the trek is over; alternatively if there are only one or two of you, you might chance getting a lift back into Dogubeyazit.

4) Mule hire in Eli village. The price of the muleteers is included in the hire charge. How many you need depends on the size of the group, and you may decide to carry your own kit. Don't forget that the guide will also have some equipment, and may be less willing to carry it!

5) Supplies. Buy in Doğubeyazit.

İşak Paşa Saray, Doğubeyazit

Starting points

The nearest town and starting point for the ascent is Doğubeyazit.
This is a drab place, being the last town in Turkey before the Iranian
border on the E23 trunk road. Besides Mount Ararat it has one major
attraction; the ruins of İşak Paşa Sarayı which reside on a dramatic
spur overlooking the town (see "other walks in the area" section).
It has all the usual supplies associated with a medium sized town.

Practical considerations

Via the easiest (S) route, Ararat is an easy snow plod, Grade 1. There
are no technical difficulties involved, the biggest obstacles being
acclimatisation and the weather. At 5137m, it is nearly 1000m higher
than any other point in Turkey. Height is gained rapidly with no
extended walk-in needed. Consequently, most ascensionists suffer
some mild symptoms of altitude sickness (see health section in
introduction). The cold winters and high altitude mean that summer
is the only practical time for most climbers - go outside these times
and you are facing serious cold problems, together with heavy
104

winter snowfall. The bulk of ascents take place in July and August.

Being high and isolated, Ararat attracts its own weather system, and the top is often shrouded in thick mist. Whilst this is unlikely to obscure the tracks of the scores of visiting climbers, it makes the summit experience less satisfying. The way to avoid this is to aim to reach the summit as early as possible.

Ice-axes are strongly recommended, crampons advisable. The track as mentioned above is likely to be well worn. Take plenty of warm gear - duvet, gloves and headwear, and don't forget sunblock cream; the ultraviolet is very intense despite the mist.

Route description

Normal route from S

Traditionally, this starts from Eli village, and is so described. However, I was informed recently by a local guide that the road to Eli had been washed out and treks now started from nearby Cevirme village. Whichever is the case, the route is substantially unaltered.

The ascent can be accomplished in three days walking; groups usually take four or five. Unless you are in a hurry, the extra time to acclimatise is worthwhile. As the shape may suggest, much of the walking is on a gentle, featureless slope. Ararat is truly one of those mountains where the summit is the only reason for setting foot upon it.

Drive from Dogubeyazit E along the main trunk road to Iran for approx. 6km to a side road on the L, which leads in 12km to Eli. You can spend the night here, but it is more usual to continue on foot for a few hours to a higher camp; the decision is unlikely to be yours.

To reach this site, known rather prosaically as camp I, leave Eli in a northerly direction along a good track, climbing diagonally leftwards up the slope, for 1hr. The motorable track ends hereabouts, but a clear path continues uphill in the same general direction. The terrain is fairly nondescript, the only point of note being the small yayla of Ibrahimkara just before the campsite. 4hrs from end of motorable track, 5hrs total. This uninspiring campsite at 3200m is usually crowded and dirty. Sadly, you may need to spend a full day here acclimatising.

Camp I to Camp II

This is a short day, taking only 3-4 hrs.

Cross from the campsite to the obvious trail over to the R (E). This leads steadily up over ever sparser vegetation and the ubiquitous obsidian boulders, following a valley side for much of the way. Eventually you emerge onto a promontory which marks the site of Camp II at 4200m. The campsite is cramped, so most parties only spend one night here. In any case, this is all that is needed, Camp I being such a short distance below in descent.

Camp II to Summit (5137m)

As mentioned previously, an early start is desirable to maximise the chances of a clear summit and view.

From Camp II, a wearisome slog through the boulder-covered slopes leads in $2^{1}/_{2}$-3hrs to the edge of the snowcap; look out for the marker post on the rocks.

Put your crampons on if you've brought them, and enjoy the feel of crisp snow under your feet. (It usually turns slushy by late morning.) Ahead lies the W peak, Inonu, with the main summit over to the R. Traverse the gentle slope beneath Inonu to gain the crevassed summit cone.

Gain the summit in 1hr or so ($3^{1}/_{2}$-4hrs total). The summit itself is graced by a small wooden ark, containing the route book. If lucky, you should be able to make out the Caucasus mountains to the N, the Kaçkar range, and the line of volcanic peaks stretching down towards Lake Van and into Iran. Closer to hand is Little Mount Ararat with its remarkably pure form.

Descent: retrace your steps, allowing at least as long to reach Camp II as in ascent. From there, Camp I is gained in a further 2hrs, and another 2hrs again to Eli. These times are approximate; John Town (see bibliography) reached Eli from Camp II in 50mins!

Other routes on Ararat
All routes listed below are currently banned; they are included in case this situation changes.

E face (Mih Tepe) route

Originally the most popular route, this started from the Aras valley to the N, via a well at Serdarbulak, then gained the col (2600m) between Great and Little Mount Ararat. From here, the route follows a stepped ridge to a noticeable rock outcrop known as Taş Kilise (lit. "stone church") at c.4000m. A long ice slope, or loose rock ridge to its L, leads to the summit.

From NW

Starting from a village on the road between Iğdır and Doğubeyazit, near its highest point, cross the extensive plateau to Kop Gölu, then up rocks to the summit.

N Face

A steep ice route, tackling the face just to the R (E) of the impressive gash of the Ahora valley.

Other walks in the Ararat area

Doğubeyazit's other main attraction, İşak paşa Sarayı, lies on a spur overlooking the town, and is at the end of a 7km metalled road. Due to its popularity, there are numerous minibuses ferrying visitors to and from town. Catch one of these, or do as I did; make an early start and walk there in 1hr 30mins or so. It is a pleasant trek through fields and grassland.

Once there, you can explore the castle and the older mosque which lies across from it on the other side of the defile. The real attraction to the visiting walker, though, lies beyond İsak Paşa Sarayı in the limestone mountains that form the backdrop.

Their lower slopes, behind the castle, are dotted in summer with the tents of Kurd holidaymakers. As everywhere in the mountains, you will find it hard to pass without being invited for tea at every tent. Climb the mountain behind the old mosque and you will be rewarded with a view of Ararat, invisible from the environs of the castle. For a gentle mountain day, with cultural and historical interest, this is hard to beat in Eastern Anatolia.

PART FIVE

Lake Van Area

The beautiful Lake Van is one of the jewels of Turkey. A large soda lake, nearly 100km wide in places, its dazzling blue colour gives it a Mediterranean aspect. Surrounding the lake are numerous mountains, generally dormant or extinct volcanoes. Of these, Suphan Dağ 4434m is the highest, somewhat resembling Mount Ararat in appearance.

This area of eastern Turkey has seen many civilisations come and go, including the Urartians, whose capital was on the outskirts of modern-day Van city.

Sadly, contemporary events are making their presence felt here also. Kurdish separatists have extended their area of operations, and the Lake Van region is now considered unsafe for travellers. Several people have been kidnapped, and whilst it is true to say that the majority (possibly all) have been released unharmed after a brief spell in captivity, it would be irresponsible to advise someone to visit the area.

When I climbed Suphan Dağ and Nemrut Dağ in the mid-1980s, it would have been hard to imagine the current situation. My memories of days spent on remote mountains in this far-flung corner of Anatolia, where the only other human presence was the occasional shepherd, make me hope that at some stage things will improve as quickly as they have deteriorated. With this in mind, I have included the following route descriptions, but stress again that up-to-date information should be obtained before entering the region.

The climate in this part of Turkey is severe, with very cold winters - the summer months from June to August are the most suitable times to visit.

Crater lake, Nemrut Dağ, Lake Van

Nemrut Dağ 3050m

Not to be confused with the better-known Nemrut Dağ in upper Mesopotamia (where the stone heads are), the chief feature of this mountain is the large crater lake in the summit caldera.

Although not impressive as a mountain, Nemrut Dağ's impact on the surrounding landscape has been profound. The eruption of Nemrut Dağ blocked the outflow river for the Van basin, forming Lake Van as we now know it.

The ascent of Nemrut Dağ is straightforward enough, and can be easily accomplished in a short day. The best starting point is the town of Tatvan, the railway and ferry terminus for services to Van city.

Head NE out of town until just beyond the outskirts. There is a dirt road which turns off L and leads up into the summit crater - it is preferable not to take this. Instead, just cut across country, aiming ever upwards until you reach the edge of the summit crater. The change in outlook is dramatic - in front of you a mile-wide crater,

109

rimmed with obsidian cliffs, and with a deep lake in the centre.

You should be able to see the road down into the crater. When I was there, several black felt Kurdish nomad tents were pitched on the lava flow near the lake. It's worth descending to the lake for a swim and to get a glimpse of traditional Kurdish culture.

Suphan Dağ 4434m

If the spot height is to be believed, this is the second highest mountain in Turkey, and like the highest, Ararat, is a conical dormant volcano. Unlike Ararat, however, there were no restrictions on access and very few foreigners ever visited the mountain. Several maps show greatly varying heights for the summit - the figure quoted seems to be close to the majority of these.

The starting point for ascents of Suphan Dağ is the small town of Adilcevaz, on the shores of Lake Van 67km north-east of Tatvan. There is little here other than an ancient castle and the very attractive Tüğrül Bey mosque. Frequent buses ply the road between here and Tatvan. There are one or two very basic hotels in town - the one I

Lakeside mosque, Adilcevaz

stayed in (which doesn't give the appearance of being a hotel) is above the bakery at the top end of the main street.

Suphan Dağ can be climbed in a day from Adilcevaz, and personally I feel that this is the best option. When I climbed Suphan Dağ, I avoided the yaylas because of the unfriendly reception I received from children. It is fair to say that the only overt hostility I ever encountered in Turkey was in this area, from kids throwing stones. It is a long hike for a day, but preferable to camping out near a village.

From Adilcevaz, the first destination is the attractive mountain lake of Aygır Gölu. This is reached by a boring, dusty road and so it makes sense to travel this section by taxi. Arrange in Adilcevaz for one to collect you in the morning, no later than 06.00. It shouldn't cost more than £5. On arriving in Aygır Gölu, skirt the lake on its LH side, and gain a grassy ridge heading directly up the slope. The rest of the route essentially follows this.

Avoiding the yaylas, continue up the ridge, which gradually becomes barer and the obsidian rock is exposed underfoot. In its upper section, the ridge peters out into a smooth slope - ascend this to gain abruptly a sharp ridge crest, often snow-covered. Ahead is an impressive sight - the inner caldera of Suphan Dağ, with two high lakes. One of these was still frozen when I visited here. Straight in front is a large scree/lava mound, with several distinct tops, whilst to the left, the ridge curves round, drops down to a col, then continues up steeply to another top. This latter top appears to be the summit, but in fact the highest point is one of the tops in the scree mound.

Drop down from the ridge, cross the valley containing the lakes, and laboriously ascend the mound opposite. The true summit is set some way back, and is not obvious. I confess that I missed it altogether when I was there, but apparently it is noticeably higher once you have ascended it! The view from here is superb, with the whole of Lake Van visible, and the mountains beyond the eastern shore extending towards Iran. Allow 7hrs or more in ascent to the summit from Aygır Gölu. Descent, following the same route, is much more rapid. With luck, as I had, you will be able to hitch a lift back from Aygır Gölu to Adilcevaz, in time for a swim in Lake Van.

Çandır Dağ seen from Akdamar island

Çandır Dağ 3537m

This mountain forms the backdrop to the small town of Gevaş, near where the ferry crosses to Akdamar Island. Despite being adjacent to Van's greatest tourist attraction, it is virtually unknown to walkers.

Akdamar Island itself is a must on anyone's itinerary. Situated a few kms offshore, there is a wonderfully preserved tenth-century Armenian church, covered in fine stone carving.

To climb Çandır Dağ, catch a bus to the town of Gevaş, set just off the main Van-Tatvan highway. Follow the river upstream, on the southern side, until it is possible to gain the ridge which descends from Çandır Dağ. This is at the point where the river valley swings round to the right (S). Follow the bare ridge to gain the summit. 4-5hrs from Gevaş. Looking S from the summit, the remote mountain ranges of Kurdistan disappear into the distance.

Descent: retrace your steps.

PART SIX

The Aladağ Range (Aladağlar)

Introduction

This is one of the finest areas for mountaineering in Turkey. Stark dolomitic peaks rising above narrow valleys or high glacial basins combine to produce a wild, dramatic scenery unsurpassed in the Taurus mountains.

It is ridge scrambler's country par excellence, with long knife-edged arêtes linking a series of tops, and sometimes providing easy routes up otherwise very difficult peaks. A day following one of these ridges can give one of the most memorable outings in Turkey.

The Aladağ range is part of the central Taurus mountains, and lies approximately midway between Kayseri and Adana, 45km east of Niğde. The area of interest to walkers is relatively compact, adding to the attraction of this as a destination. This area is strictly speaking called the Beyaz Aladağ, to distinguish it from the more rolling hills of the Siyah Aladağ. The name "Ala Dağ" can be translated variously as "pink" or "crimson" mountains, but an alternative explanation is "high mountains". This would make sense of the prefixes "Beyaz" (white) and "Siyah" (black).

In summer the upper valleys and high basins are home to Yoruk families, who continue an age-old way of life.

The relative ease of access, the compact nature of the area, and quality of climbing have ensured the Ala Dağ range's popularity with Turkish mountaineers. In recent years, the area has also become popular with Western trekkers. Numbers visiting are still small, and it is easy to get away into remote valleys where groups have never been seen.

The Aladağlar are wooded on the eastern and southern slopes, but the over-riding impression is of an arid, karstic landscape. There is permanent snow in basins and couloirs, but no glaciers as such; evidence of past glaciation is abundant.

A welcome recent addition to the literature is *The Ala Dağ* by

113

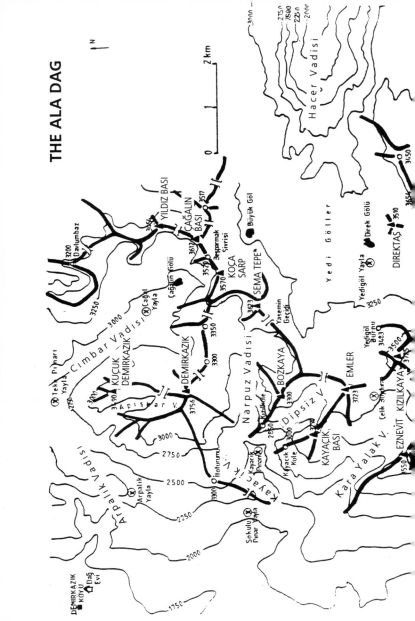

THE ALA DAG

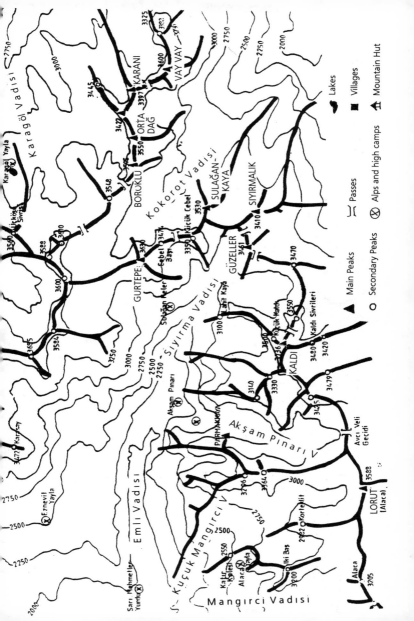

Ömer Tüzel. Also published by Cicerone Press, this gives more detailed information on climbing routes in the Aladağlar. In this chapter I have tried to use the same nomenclature as in Ömer's book.

Maps

Until very recently, none were commercially available. A 1:25,000 map has been produced by Bozkurt Ergör. Trek Travel also produce a map based on this. Both maps suffer from poor coverage of the southern part of the range. Various sketch maps exist in the mountaineering literature, of variable quality. As elsewhere in Turkey, considerable confusion exists as to nomenclature on these maps. However, a 1:25,000 scale map is now commercially available from: Geo Agentur, Verlag für geographische, thematische Medien, Paul Heyselstr. Nr. 23, 8000 München 2, Germany.

Useful contacts and addresses

There are several guides operating in the Aladağlar. One of these is Ali Şafak, who speaks good English. He is to be found at his guest house, situated at the Çukurbağ turnoff from the main Niğde-Çamardı road (see below). If you do not require his services as a guide, he is a mine of information, and can arrange mule hire.

The principal areas

Although compact in size, the Aladaglar consists of several distinct areas, each with its own character.

To describe these, it is most sensible to start with the great central plateau/basin of Yedigöller. From here the main areas are:

1)   To the NW, the Cımbar Valley
2)   To the W, Sokullupınar, the Narpuz and Yalak gorges
3)   To the SW, the Emli Valley. Kaldı, Güzeller and Alaca
4)   To the SE, the Torasan area - Acıman, the Kokorot Valley, and Karagöl - including Yedigöller, a total of five principal areas, and they are described separately in this book.

Approaches and starting points

There are three main approaches, of which the first described is by far the most popular and convenient.

1)   From NW (Niğde, Kayseri)

From Niğde, frequent buses lead to the village of Çukurbağ, at the foot of the Aladağ and the starting point for nearly all treks. (NB. the final destination of the buses is usually the nearby large village of Çamardı, which has basic shops, banks and post office.)

Çukurbağ (alt. c.1480 m) has very few facilities. At the turn-off from the main Niğde-Çamardı road, there is a small pension, newly opened, run by the Şafak brothers. A few hundred metres further up the road towards Çamardı is a petrol station with small kebab house attached - beer is also served here. Shopping is best done in Niğde.

2km before Çukurbağ (when approaching from Niğde) lies the village of Demirkazık, situated, as the name suggests, below the slopes of Demirkazık peak. At the head of the village is a large mountain refuge and ski centre. Principally used in the winter, it is open throughout the year. It offers dormitory and bedroom accommodation and meals. Prices are rather steep (£12 half-board). Demirkazık is really only useful for access to the Cımbar valley (see later description).

2)   From E (Yahyalı)

Infrequent minibuses run from Yahyalı to Barazama (poor shopping). This village gives access to Yedigöller and Karagöl/Acıman areas. There are no pensions in the village at present, but asking around should result in some accommodation being offered.

Buses also run from Yahyalı to Şelale village, near Barazama. This is a good starting point for Acıman and the Kokorot Valley.

3)   From S (Karşantı)

This approach has little to commend it, unless you are heading specifically for the southern part of the range. Rough roads, just passable by minibus but more suited to tractors, lead to the mineral spring at Acıman. Tractors can be hired for the journey in Karşantı.

Acıman itself consists of nothing other than a spring in a high pasture below Torasan peak. There are no other facilities, or anywhere to leave excess baggage. Several yaylas surround this area in high summer. It is, however, the best starting point for walks and climbs in the southern part of the range. It can be reached more easily from Barazama (see routes from Barazama).

List of Peaks

This list includes the major Aladağ peaks in order of height, but not minor tops. The names in brackets are synonyms which occur in the climbing literature. The given heights vary on some maps.

1)	Demirkazık	3756m
2)	Kızılkaya	3725m
3)	Embler (Emler, Emli Basi)	3723m
4)	Kaldı	3688m
5)	Kızılyar	3654m
6)	Gürtepe	3630m
7)	Sematepe	3623m
8)	Tosun Tepe (Çağalın Bası)	3612m
9)	Torasan	3584m
10)	Alaca (Alacı Başı, Lorut, Ludut Dağ)	3582m
11)	Vay-Vay Dağ	3563m
12)	Boruklu	3548m
13)	Sulağankaya	3530m
14)	Direktaş	3510m
15)	Ortadağ (Mystery peak)	3500m
16)	Cebelbaşı	3474m
17)	Karasay	3472m
18)	Güzeller	3461m
19)	Sıyırmalik (C1)	3426m
20)	Küçük Demirkazık	3400m

N.B. Throughout the text, "Demirkazık" refers to the peak, rather than the village of that name.

Sokullupınar area

This is the closest area to Çukurbağ, and is often the first stopping point for visitors.

Sokullupınar itself lies at the entrance to the Narpuz gorge, a deep cleft in the mountain wall separating Demirkazık from Embler, which leads into an attractive high valley. The area is dominated by Demirkazık (3756m).

Whilst there are limited day hikes and climbs from Sokullupınar, it lies en route to Yedigöller, and many parties continue after spending just one night here. This is a pity, as there is much to see from here.

A disadvantage of Sokullupınar as a base for ascending peaks is the low altitude - c.2020m.

AL1 Approach - Çukurbağ to Sokullupınar

As mentioned above, Sokullupınar lies at the entrance to the Narpuz Gorge, which provides a good means of locating the site. There is a motorable track which leads up to Sokullupınar from Demirkazık village (4 wheel drive preferable). It is possible to arrange for a taxi to drop gear here from Çamardı.

From Çukurbağ - head up east through orchards to gain a track after 10 minutes on right (true L) bank of a small ravine leading up towards Demirkazık.

Follow this line for 20mins to a bifurcation - take L branch towards Demirkazık peak. Emerge to fine views of Embler and the western flanks of Demirkazık. The prominent cleft ahead is the Narpuz Gorge; Çelikbuyduran is the next break on the right, leading to Yedigöller. To the far right can be seen Alaca and associated peaks on the far side of the Emlı valley.

After 45mins, head NE across a grassy upland, with the Narpuz Gorge on your right. In another 10mins (55mins total) reach a motorable track heading N. Take this, leaving it where it turns left back down towards the main valley.

Up to twin boulders, which provide welcome shade in summer.

Back E up a broad ridge to reach a viewpoint overlooking Sokullupinar on the left bank of the dry river, below the foot of Narpuz Gorge.

Drop down into the dry river valley (the Yalak Deresı), mainly dry with one or two small springs in mid summer. Up the other bank to reach Sokullupınar (2hrs 50mins).

Trek Travel have a permanent camp here, on the best available site. A concrete water trough with good drinkable water lies 100m down from here by the motor track. There are camping sites further up towards the gorge mouth, or 20mins higher on the track above the river bed towards Çelikbuyduran.

Excursions from Sokullupınar

AL2 Sokullupınar to Narpuz Gorge

This route, which passes through some impressive rock scenery leads to the head of the Narpuz valley, a good base for ascents of Demirkazık. In the initial parts of the gorge at least it is impossible to get lost!

It is possible to link this route with the hike to Dipsiz Göl via the difficult Demirkazık pass - see routes AL3 and AL6.

Head to the base of the cleft and ascend the steep ravine (easy walk/scramble) heading roughly E-W. After 25mins this opens out into a fine cirque, with the complex flanks of Demirkazık forming the L wall. Immediately up on the R is an area of grassy slopes known as Kayacık. There is a spring and, occasionally, a solitary yayla here.

Follow the broader valley bottom, which is easier angled. The stream dries up after a few hundred metres. Continue along the dry gravel river bed, whose broadness suggests that a large volume of water flows here in springtime.

1hr 15mins leads to the base of a very narrow cleft, which is the start of a difficult gorge. Circumventing this is the most difficult part of the route. Don't try to climb directly up the gorge - in mid-July this is still blocked by snowdrifts. Instead, take an intermittent track up onto slabs on L (true R). Route finding is difficult here - it is possible to traverse without any difficult scrambling, but great care is needed, both in route finding and on account of loose gravel on bare rock. Exposed. Ascend till level with the top of a large verdant patch at the head of the gorge, on opposite bank, then contour horizontally as best you can. 2hrs 20mins.

Reach the end of ravine, and continue up the now easier valley which ends in another 50mins or so. There are two possible exits - N via the Demirkazık pass to Dipsiz Göl (q.v.) and the Cımbar valley; and via Yaşemin Pass SE to Yedigöller basin (q.v.)

AL2A The Dipsiz Vadı

This valley, which lies to the S and W of the upper Narpuz valley, affords a possible route over to the Yedigöller basin, emerging on the ridge N of Embler via a col. The disadvantage of this route is the pathless slog up scree to gain the upper reaches of the valley. Virtually never visited, it is a good place to see Caspian snowcock, and with a decent snow covering could be worth trying.

AL3 Sokullupınar to Cımbar Valley and Dipsiz Göl

From Sokullupınar head N roughly parallel to the cliff base. (A road snakes up to the mouth of a cave at the base of the cliff.) Gain the dirt road on the skyline and follow this. Behind, the southern peaks appear in view. After 40mins the valley leading into the Cımbar valley proper comes into view, and Demirkazık village is visible below.

Where the road snakes back down to Demirkazık village, continue right ahead over a small depression heading NE (50mins) towards the now prominent deep valley. Küçük Demirkazık is now clearly distinguishable from Demirkazık to its right. As you skirt a gorge down below to your L, rather than descend into the valley bottom continue up to the cliff bottom and the small yayla of Arpalık (spring here). The friendly inhabitants were making delicious hot bread turnovers filled with cheese and herbs last time I visited here.

From Arpalık take the high track on the hillside, which affords fine views of the gorge below. Continue up the valley, passing beneath the immaculate grey limestone slabs of Küçük Demirkazık, to reach a small col (2hrs 15mins) with the Cımbar Valley just ahead.

The ridge immediately to NW of the col provides a worthwhile detour for the fine views.

Descend on a good path from the right-hand side of the col to the valley bottom, where there is a good, reliable spring and one or two flat camping spots (this is shown on maps as Teke Pınarı, and is the junction with the path up from Demirkazık village). Immediately down from here, the Cımbar Valley becomes a narrow steep-sided gorge. This has been developed recently as a hard rock climbing area by Turkish climbers.

From Teke Pınarı, follow the valley bottom as for the Demirkazık village - Dipsiz Göl route as far as the lake (3hrs 30mins) - described in the Dipsiz Göl/Cımbar Valley section.

AL4 Sokullupınar to Emli Valley

NB. The quickest way of reaching the Emli Valley is direct from Çukurbağ - see description in Emli Valley section.

From Sokullupınar take the path above the camp which trends rightwards above the dry Yatak deresı, towards the mouth of the prominent weakness which marks the start of the Çelikbuyduran pass (q.v.). Continue as for Çelikbuyduran to just before where this route passes below the first rock buttress. Ascend the steep grassy hillside via an intermittent path which heads diagonally back left, towards the end of the mud/rock pinnacles. Emerge onto a subsidiary ridge near a ridge with a rocky buttress, 150m to the L. (40mins).

Up the subsidiary ridge to a junction with the main ridge and continue in this direction to emerge after 55mins onto a grassy upland (Tulutepe, 2139m) with views of the south bounding ridge of Alaca and associated peaks. There is a good view back to the SW face of Demirkazık. Heading roughly S, skirt the rocky bowl on its upper side, and join a proper track near a saddle with a prominent conical mound on its R.

Continue to the saddle which is deceptively far (1hr 40mins). This overlooks the Emli Valley and gives fine views of peaks including the magnificent Kaldı, which rivals Demirkazık in its grandeur. Near this saddle, approximately 50m before it, is an unsuspected and well hidden concreted trough. This is known as

Eznevit, and occasionally supports a small yayla. (NB. the substantial yayla seen below on the floor of the Emli Valley is often erroneously referred to in the literature as Eznevit.) From the saddle head gently down ESE then traverse the steep hillside on a decent path, which gradually loses height and eventually descends down to the valley bottom, below a large yayla situated on a glacial moraine (2hrs 30mins).

Just before the yayla is reached, the very impressive 150m high rock pinnacle known as Parmakkaya (lit. "rock finger") comes into view to the S. This has been ascended at least twice, but, at the time of writing, still offers immense potential for new routes.

Slightly lower than Parmakkaya lies the spring of Akşampinari (lit. "evening spring"). This is difficult to find, but it supplies the large yayla via a pipe.

The Cımbar Valley and Dipsiz Göl

This valley delineates the northernmost part of the Aladağ range. Rocky and narrow, the main attraction is as a base for ascents of Demirkazık. At the head of the valley lies the beautiful Dipsiz Göl (lit. "enclosed lake") set in a cirque of fine rock walls. Dipsiz Göl is also known as Çağalın Göl. In early summer, the floor of this cirque is carpeted with wild crocus and squill.

Other than by the few climbers who are tackling Demirkazık, the area is little visited, and makes an idyllic camping spot. The valley makes a suitable base for the ascent of Demirkazık (including the North Face) and Küçük Demirkazık. At its lower end, the valley enters a narrow gorge, which debouches above Demirkazık village.

There is a choice of campsites; Dipsiz Göl is the most attractive and obvious, but rather too far up the valley for ascending Demirkazık. In the latter case, green patches by a spring 30mins walk before Dipsiz Göl provide a suitable site.

Although the approach from Demirkazık village is described, the Cımbar valley is reached just as easily from Çukurbağ via Sokullupinar (see "excursions from Sokullupınar" section, route AL4).

AL5 Approach - Demirkazık village to Dipsiz Göl

From Demirkazık village, follow the signs to the Kayak Evi ("Ski House"). Continue along a good track in a SE direction. After twenty minutes, the track splits - straight ahead to Arpalık yayla, the LH path to the lower Cımbar gorge. The former is a better path, but is slightly more roundabout; the latter takes you NE then E through the impressive rock scenery of the gorge. Both will lead to the small spring and yayla of Teke Pınarı, in 2hrs 30mins from Demirkazık.

A few minutes further on, the valley turns right revealing the peaks at the head of the valley to ESE. Reach another spring after 2hrs 40mins. The valley continues to curve to the right, skirting the foot of Küçük Demirkazık.

After 3hrs the valley opens out and reveals the majestic peak of Demirkazık to the SSW which comes fully into view as you continue.

There is a nice campsite here, and an even more idyllic one further on, providing a good base for ascents of Demirkazık. The E ridge of Demirkazık forms the left-hand skyline of the peak, and leads down to an obvious notch which is Demirkazık Pass.

To continue to Dipsiz Göl head up the main valley for a further 30mins, through masses of alpine flowers to the lake (2,900m), which is well hidden until the last (3hrs 30mins). This is magnificently situated with snow banks descending to the water's edge from the large crags which surround it. The only weakness in the cirque is to the NE where an easy angled slope leads up to a pass over to Yıldız Gölu (q.v.).

Demirkazık 3756m from Cımbar Valley

For an ascent of Demirkazık, the ideal campsite is 30mins below Dipsiz Göl, rather than at the lake itself. There are several possible routes; only the standard E ridge route is feasible for scramblers.

AL6 Demirkazık E ridge Grade II

The most popular route up the mountain, and possibly in the whole of the Aladağlar. Not to be missed by a competent party. It is quite possible to do the route without any special climbing equipment, but the airiness of the ridge needs a good head for heights. The route described here joins up with the normal E ridge route at a col on the ridge, the Demirkazık Geçidi (pass).

From the campsite down from Dipsiz Göl, head towards the summit of Demirkazik. The skyline ridge descending to the L from the summit is the E ridge - aim for the prominent notch.

Skirt round a spur and up into the cwm below Demirkazık. Aim for the gully, which is mainly scree. This is unpleasant, but it steepens towards the top, and becomes more solid (moves of II). It is best to keep on the right side of the gully. Gain the top of the col after 2¹/₂-3hrs from the campsite. (NB. In early season, the gully is snow-filled, necessitating ice-axe and crampons. This is more pleasant than when scree-filled, however.)

The normal E ridge route is joined here. Follow slabby rock, keeping to the R, until the ridge proper is attained. This broadens near the summit, and becomes easier. Allow 1-1¹/₂hrs from col to summit. The view, as you would expect, is magnificent, with most of the Aladağlar peaks visible.

In descent, retrace your steps, taking care to keep to the L (as looking ahead), and allow as long as for the ascent.

AL7 Dipsiz Göl to Yıldız Göl and Tekkekalesı

This stage can be combined with the next one to Yedigöller; this would involve crossing a ridge at c.3500m, and gives a long day. From Dipsiz Göl, head up E to the only obvious weakness in the surrounding cwm wall. Gain the pass top after an hour's toil up easy scree. From here, descend down to the patch of green and one or two small lakes; this is the attractively named Yıldız Göl ("star lake"). There are occasionally one or two Yoruk tents here. This is the best camping spot this side of Yedigöller, but if you have only crossed from Dipsiz Göl, this might be too short a day. As mentioned above, you can either carry on to Yedigöller ($5^{1}/_{2}$-6hrs from here), or ascend Tekkekalesi and return to camp. Part of the ascent is shared with the route over to Yedigöller, however!

Looking south from the Yildiz Göl area, there is a deep valley formed by the ridge (actually the back wall of Dipsiz Göl) on the R and the whaleback of Tekkekalesı on the L.

Follow this valley, skirting under the cliffs of Tekkekalesı, to reach a point where the cliffs of Tekkekalesı drop back. It is possible to climb a long scree slope up to the col between Tekkekalesı and a rocky spur descending from the main bounding ridge. Either follow the ridge up to the summit of Tekkekalesı, or:

AL7A Continuation to Yedigöller

Take the rocky spur, mainly on its L, without any difficulty to reach the ridge top at a point just below Pt 3517m, and with a magnificent vista of Yedigöller ahead.

Alternatively, it is possible to skirt round to the L (E) side of Tekkekalesı and ascend to the col; this is longer and of lesser scenic interest.

From Pt 3517m, head W a short way along the ridge crest then descend easy scree slopes to arrive at the beautiful lakes and meadows of Hasta Hocanin yaylası, in the Yedigöller basin.

Walking up to the entrance of the Emlı Valley. Alaca straight ahead, the Mangırcı Valley up and right

The Emlı Valley area

This beautiful valley provides the main base for exploring the southernmost peaks of the Aladağ. These include Alaca, Kaldı and Güzeller, together with a host of other rock peaks. As such it affords sufficient scope for several days or even weeks of mountaineering. In its lower reaches the Emlı Valley is thinly forested with conifers - the only valley on the western flanks of Aladağ so blessed. Despite the trees, there is little available water.

In addition, it provides the quickest access to the Vay-Vay/Torasan range when approaching from the West.

From the West, the Emlı Valley is best approached via a motorable track which leads from Çukurbağ village almost to the mouth of the valley. It can also be reached (slightly longer) from Sokullupınar - see Sokullupınar section, route AL4.

AL8 Emlı Valley from Çukurbağ

From the road junction, walk down the road towards Çukurbağ, take the right turn, and follow this road through the village, past the mosque.

A new road crosses the barren hillside, leading towards the mouth of the Emlı Valley. At any junctions, keep on the main or RH road, to reach a point after 2hrs or so where the road drops down to the dry river bed. (It is easier and preferable to avoid this dull section by taking a taxi to here. Cost from Çamardı £7, from Çukurbağ £3.50.)

From here the path continues along the valley floor. Pass a beekeeper's hut (usually) after a few hundred metres, and a short way beyond this, a curious rock tomb cut in a huge boulder.

Just before the narrows lies the Yayla of Sarımehmetler, and on the other side of the narrows a large concreted trough (safe to drink).

The Mangırcı valley lies off to the R from here; the main valley continues with a bend to the L and enters an area of pine forest. Pleasant walking through this, on a prominent track, leads to the large yayla below Parmakkaya. 5hrs walking from Çukurbağ, 3hrs with taxi.

The side valley which leads S from here, past Parmakkaya leads to the Auçiveli pass and the southern flanks of the Aladağlar.

Continuing up the main valley, which curves round slightly to the ESE, leads to where it abruptly finishes in a series of steep snow-filled cwms flanked by subsidiary ridges descending from the main peaks. There are some good camping sites here.

Excursions from Emlı Valley

AL9 Auçiveli Pass 3170m

This pass, as previously mentioned, leads to the southern side of the Aladag range. It is also used as an approach to Alaca and Kaldı.

From the large yayla in the valley bottom, head up the side valley, steeply at first, past Parmakkaya, to reach a shallow basin (1hr). Continue up this, following the valley round to the L, until the Auçiveli pass is visible ahead (1hr 30min).

Another 45mins leads to the summit of the pass at approximately

The lower reaches of the Narpuz gorge
Direktas

The river between Barazama and Şelale
Emergent river at Şelale

The entrance to the Mangırcı Valley

3170m. There can be steep snow on this last section early in the season. From the summit the Bolkar Taurus can be discerned in the distance to the SW.

AL10 Alaca 3582m via E ridge Grade II

This is the standard route, and provides an easy, though airy, ridge walk, with a very short scrambling section.

From the Auçiveli pass, head westwards on easy scree, keeping to the L (S) side of the ridge, bypassing some rock outcrops, to the ridge crest. Easily along this, with a small scrambling section at a little chimney, to gain the summit via a couple of subsidiary tops. The N face (apparently unclimbed) is extremely impressive when seen from this angle. (2hrs from Auçiveli, 3¼-3¾hrs from Emli Valley).

Descent: via the same route. Allow 3hrs.

AL11 Alaca 3582m via West ridge Grade II and Mangırcı Valley

Similar in character to the previous route, though with rather more scrambling. The initial approach is via the unfrequented Mangırcı Valley, which is well worth a visit in itself.

To reach the Mangırcı Valley, it is best to approach directly from Cukurbag, taking the road into the Emlı Valley. The route from Sokullupınar arrives further up this valley, and would necessitate back-tracking.

On the approach from Çukurbağ, there is a prominent rock peak, Kaletepe. This delineates the Eastern side of the Mangırcı Valley. Below Kaletepe, where the Mangırcı Valley enters the main Emlı Valley, lies the Sarimehmetler spring. This provides a convenient reference point, as well as making a good (though low) base.

From here, follow a path which leads into the Mangırcı Valley, gaining height, to reach a ridge which descends from Alaca, dividing the upper valley into two. Take the RH (westernmost) branch, skirting under the dividing ridge, until at the head of the valley, an ascent can be made to a point where this ridge joins the main watershed ridge (4-4½hrs).

The upper reaches of this valley is one of the few places where Caspian snowcock are likely to be seen in the Aladağ.

AL12 Un-named peak c.3100m

This peak is situated on the terminal ridge descending into the Emlı Valley from Pt 3440m. This is the next ridge beyond the E-bounding ridge of the Parmakkaya valley, when seen from the lower Emlı Valley. Although I have not climbed this peak, or read of any ascents in the available literature, this looks to be an interesting short route.

The best means of ascent would appear to be to gain the saddle between this peak and Pt 3440m from the W, then to follow the ridge crest to the summit.

Kaldı 3723m

This magnificent peak is one of the finest in the Aladağ. The main peak is surrounded by several satellite peaks.

There are several routes on Kaldı; only the easiest, being within the capabilities of a walker, is described here.

Kaldı as seen on approach to Çebelbası-Gürtepe ridge

AL13 Kaldı via W ridge Grade II

This is the normal means of ascent, and by far the easiest. The route essentially follows the main ridge from the Auçiveli pass E to the summit.

This is a long ascent, and as steps are retraced on the descent, it is sensible to establish a high camp up towards the Auçiveli pass. It can be done in a long day from Akşampınarı, however. Either gain the summit of the Auçiveli pass (3170m), or take the prominent subsidiary cwm to the L (E), which allows the main ridge to be gained more directly.

In either case, follow the main ridge E, easily, towards a point where the ridge turns N, through nearly 90 degrees. The route continues along the ridge, passing the point where the more direct start joins it, and skirts beneath an outlying satellite known as Kaldı Bası. (The satellite peak itself can be reached by some easy [grade II] scrambling.) Gain the obvious broad scree/snow plateau between this outlier and the main summit.

Continue towards the main summit. Between this and a subsidiary top just to its R (S) is a col; gain this (snow in early season) then follow a rock crest on the L. This involves a short scrambling section (Grade II), but it soon relents, and the summit is quickly reached. 5hrs 30mins from Auçiveli; slightly less via direct route.

Güzeller 3461m

This fine peak dominates the view at the head of the upper Emlı Valley.

AL14 Güzeller via SW ridge Grade II

The best starting point is Sulağan spring. (If you can find it!) Between Güzeller and Kaldı lies the Güzeller basin. Ascend towards this basin, skirting around the Western spur that descends from Güzeller. Once this is turned, gain a scree slope on the main bounding ridge to the E, close to where this meets the Western spur. Ascend this to a narrow gully, which leads (grade II scrambling) up to a brèche in the main ridge. Follow the ridge L to the summit without difficulty. (5hrs from main valley below Güzeller basin to summit; allow $2^{1}/_{2}$-3hrs for descent.)

AL15 Güzeller via E face Grade II

This route ascends from the brèche between Güzeller and Sıyırmalık (see photo). The main difficulty consists of a steep snow gully.

From the brèche, climb the E face to gain the large snow slope; up this to its top, where it steepens. From here, easy rocks lead easily to the summit. 5hrs from main valley to summit.

The two routes combined would make a good traverse of the mountain, easiest if ascending via the E face route.

AL16 Sıyırmalık 3426m

Another fine looking peak lying just E of Güzeller, and separated from it by a narrow col. One of the most difficult peaks in the Aladağ range. When approaching from Emlı Valley, the peak remains hidden behind its taller neighbour.

The normal route of ascent is reportedly via an unpleasant gully on the S face, reached from the brèche between Güzeller and Sıyırmalık.

The elusive Sıyırmalık, as seen from Kuçuk Cebel. The ascent gully is directly below the summit. Sulağan Kaya the nearer peak on left of picture

Cebelbaşı 3474m, Gürtepe 3630m

These peaks lie on the same ridge, which delineates the eastern boundary of the Emlı Valley. They can be reached from the col which provides a means of access to the Kokorot Valley and southern Aladağ peaks.

Gürtepe is a major peak, but Cebelbaşı is fairly nondescript; the main attraction is the magnificent view of the rarely visited Vay-Vay/Torasan area. The peaks share a common approach, and are described as such.

AL17 Cebelbaşı-Gürtepe ridge Grade II

Starting from Sulağan spring, head SE, skirting the spur which descends from Gürtepe, then turn this to head up leftwards into the cwm.

Aim for the back wall between Çebelbası (not obvious) and the summit of Gürtepe. Climb up over scree and short rock steps, to reach the summit crest. 2hrs. A further hour leads up to the summit of Gürtepe to the NW. Cebelbaşı can be reached from the same point on the ridge in approx 10mins. In descent, take care to find the correct departure point.

The ascent to the ridge is not very pleasant, and a longer but more enjoyable alternative is to gain the col leading to the Kokorot Valley, as described in route AL19. This probably adds only 30-40mins on to the trip. Easy ridge walking and scrambling N leads quickly to Cebelbaşı. From here, Gürtepe is a further 1-1$^{1}/_{2}$ hrs along the ridge. 2hrs from col.

AL18 Karasay 3472m Grade I (with continuation to Eznevit 3550m)

This peak lies on the northern side of the Emlı Valley, approximately due N of Akşampınarı. Its central location affords good views of the main Kaldı massif, and as such is a worthwhile reconnaissance trip.

From Akşampınarı, head up the prominent scree slope due N, one of the longer and more tedious Aladağ scree slogs. Take the LH side of the scree to gain the main bounding ridge at a col (2-2$^{1}/_{2}$hrs). Follow this W, then S, to reach the summit quickly and easily, at maximum 15mins beyond the col.

It is possible to continue NE along the main valley-bounding ridge to reach the summit of Eznevit, 3550m, in a further 30-40mins.

AL19 Emlı Valley to Kokorot Valley

Rather than taking the col as described in route AL17, it is easier to take the next col S, which is on the ridge just S of the Cebelbaşı summit, between it and a small peak known as Küçük Cebel, 3300m.

When approaching from Sulağan, skirt round the foot of the ridge descending from Gürtepe as for the previous route, but then head up into the SE corner of the cwm, where the lowest point on the ridge marks the col.

Ascend easily up scree to gain the col. A worthwhile detour here is to ascend Küçük Cebel due S - excellent views. From the col, descend E down into the Kokorot Valley. 4hrs from Sulağan.

Looking from the Küçük Cebel, the big rock peak in the foreground is Sulagankaya; to its R and tucked behind is Sıyırmalık; to the R of this is Güzeller. The line of peaks on the opposite side of the Kokorot Valley are the Torosan - Vay Vay group.

Other exits from Emlı Valley

1)   N over the main bounding ridge and follow this round W into Yedigöller basin. (This is as described in reverse in the Yedigöller section, route AL26.)

2)   Via a pass immediately E of Güzeller, in the SE most corner of the valley system. This is possible, but it has steep snow - avoid it in early season, and only attempt with ice-axe. It leads easily down to Çadıroğlu Yayla and then E to Acıman.

3)   N onto the main bounding ridge, then along this E, until it is possible to descend straightforwardly down slopes (from near the point of arrival of route AL26 as described in Yedigöller section) to the head of the southerly branch of the Karagöl Deresı. This has the attraction over the normal route from Emlı Valley to Kokorot and Karagöl of maintaining height.

4)   Immediately to the E of the NE ridge of Kaldı, approached from the cwm, leading up to the ridge between Kaldı and Güzeller, and forming Kaldı's SE ridge (see photo p131) is a weakness in the line of encircling cliffs. An ice-axe is needed until late summer for the northern slopes. Once on the ridge, it is a straightforward descent to the contouring path at the foot of the Aladağ's southern slopes which leads E to Acıman.

Yedigöller area

Yedigöller (lit. "seven lakes") is the name of the unique high basin surrounded by peaks in the centre of the Aladağ range, at an altitude of between 3000m and 3250m. Heavily glaciated in the past, bare rock alternates with large patches of snow which remain through to late summer. Meltwater from these feeds the numerous crystal-clear lakes which are such an attractive feature of Yedigöller. There are many more than the name suggests, although towards the end of summer several of them dry out.

Yedigöller's central location and high altitude makes it a good base for ascending several of the surrounding peaks. On this account, it is an area no visitor to the Aladağlar should miss.

In form, the basin consists of an undulating, glacially-worn plane, sloping down to the E, and divided centrally by a rounded rock mound c.150m high.

The southern flanks of Yedigöller are bounded by the vertical N face of Kızılyar, which forms a long, continuous rock wall. This curves round into a sharp ridge at its western end, forming the edge of a subsidiary basin (Latır Kırı) adjoining Yedigöller in its SW corner. This skyline ridge provides one of the best walks in the whole Taurus mountains.

Despite the level appearance of the basin when seen from above, the myriad mounds and hollows mean it is an easy place in which to become lost; a compass is advisable.

Physically, the most distinctive feature of Yedigöller is the Dolomitic rock spire of Direktaş (3510m), which is adjacent to, but detached from the main ridge at the W end of Kızılyar. Below this at Direktaş' NW corner lies Direk Göl, (or Büyük Göl), the largest lake in the basin.

Yedigöller's altitude means it is at the upper limit for grazing. In early summer here the patches of recent snowmelt are dense with wild crocus and allium. By midsummer, the snow has receded sufficiently to allow a Yoruk family to ascend with their sheep and goats, following a centuries-old tradition. The recent contact with western trekking groups has in no way affected their hospitality, and being invited to drink tea in their black tent, with Direktaş as a stunning backdrop, is one of the highlights of many a visitor's trip.

It is worth pointing out that Yedigöller suffers a severe climate, and even in midsummer it can be bitterly cold at night, with an ever-present wind blowing. As an indication of the severity, the Yoruk family arrive in mid-July and only stay for two months before the first snows force their retreat.

Campsites

There are two main areas, the first of these being the most popular. This is the area around and immediately W of Direk Göl. Direk Göl itself is unmistakable, but another landmark is a part-finished mountain hut on a hill just to the N of the lake. Apparently it has remained in this state for the last fifteen years at least, and seems unlikely ever to be finished.

On the grassy banks of the smaller lakes just to the N of Direk Göl is where both the Yoruk family and trekking groups usually stay. The view here is magnificent, the ground flat and comfortable, and the water is drinkable.

The resident cook at the Trek Travel camp sells beer to members of the tour groups; possibly he may be willing to sell to other trekkers.

If, however, you wish to enjoy the solitude of Yedigöller, there is a much nicer campsite at Hasta Hocanin Yaylası, 1hr's walk due N of the previous site. A collection of several lakes surrounded by grassy turf, they are rarely visited.

To reach Hasta Hocanin Yaylası: from the main campsite, head due N, to the L of a small conical hill, passing a small lake after 20mins or so. Pass another small lake, then descend (heading just E of N) to two large lakes, either of which provides good camping. (1hr from main campsite, 2hrs from summit of Çelikbuyduran pass.)

There are two standard approaches to the Yedigöller basin;

1.   From W - Çukurbağ/Sokullupınar via Çelikbuyduran Pass.
2.   From E - From Barazama via Soğuk Pınar and the Hacer Boğazı (valley)

AL20 Sokullupınar via Çelikbuyduran Pass to Yedigöller

This can be done in a day from Çukurbağ but this involves over 1900m of ascent and would be an exhausting first day.

The Çelikbuyduran Pass takes the obvious deep valley to the SE of Sokullupınar - as such, route finding should present few problems. Despite the steepness of parts of the gorge, this is an old trade route and is regularly taken by mules.

From Sokullupınar keep left of the Yalak river bed following a well worn path (upstream) and passing a piped spring after 40mins. This path leads through a small area of malachite, on the opposite bank of the Yalak Deresı to the prominent rock/mud pinnacles. This area is the haunt of the blue rock thrush.

The valley soon starts to narrow and steepen and after 1hr 40mins assumes the proportions of a narrow gorge. Where this is divided, take the R hand branch and follow the mule track steeply upwards. Continue up the scree filled valley bottom, skirting the S face of Embler. Worthy of note on this face is a prominent large pinnacle with a tunnel through its base. The summit of the pass remains hidden as the valley turns round to L. Eventually, after 5hrs a large spring and a stony campsite is reached, 800m before the summit of the pass.

The view from the summit is rather disappointing - the N ridge of Embler curves round to the Yaşemin Pass and Pt 3623m, which dominates the view northwards and forms the northern boundary of the Yedigöller basin. Immediately to the right of the pass are the impressive cliffs of Kızılkaya (3725m), which is a difficult, technical climb from this side.

For those who still have the energy after the long ascent, Embler (3723m) is an easy walk from the summit of the pass. Take the ridge on the left (NW) which runs down to the pass and follow this, with occasional diversions onto the right-hand scree slope to reach the top after c.45mins. Views to SE are restricted by the bulk of Kızılkaya, but to the N there is a fine view of Demirkazık. Descent: either retrace your steps to the top of the pass or, more directly, straight down scree slopes to Yedigöller.

Alternatively, it is possible to do a complete traverse of Embler by continuing N along the ridge as far as the obvious notch of the

Yaşemin Pass, although the length makes this more suitable as a day excursion from Yedigöller.

Continuing down from the summit of the pass, take the path down through scree and curve round to the E and the Yedigöller basin (1hr from summit of pass, 6hrs 15mins total).

The usual campsite is clearly visible from this descent, situated by a series of shallow ponds in a large patch of green turf.

AL21 Barazama via Hacer Valley to Yedigöller

This route is described in reverse from Yedigöller, route AL29. In ascent, the deep Hacer Valley makes route-finding very easy. The only possibility of error lies at the start, where the track heads up the hillside from Barazama. If in doubt, ask a villager. Once the track proper is gained, this leads to the motorable track in the bottom of the Hacer Valley .

Day Excursions from Yedigöller

AL22 The traverse of Embler 3723m

An easy walk, with good views.

From Yedigöller, retrace your steps as far as the summit of the Çelikbuyduran pass. From here, follow the ridge crest, with diversions on to the E (RH side) scree slopes, to attain the summit easily (45mins from pass). From the summit, continue N along the ridge, with ever finer views of Demirkazık. There is a subsidiary ridge which heads back down into the Yedigöller basin. Either descend this (easy and direct on its RH side), or much better, continue along the main ridge to the obvious col of the Yaşemin pass. Follow the ridge round to gain the summit of Pt 3623m. The ridge which heads back down to Yedigöller terminates very steeply - instead, descend the long scree slope which leads down from just below the summit, on the RH side of this ridge, to the main basin.

AL23 Pt 3517m (with continuation to Tosun Tepe 3612m)

Pt 3517m is a point on the fairly level north bounding ridge of the Yedigöller basin. It is much more interesting than its initial appearance suggests, and is an easy one-day round trip from

Yedigöller. The possible continuation along the SE ridge to Tosun Tepe (Çagalin Bası) is easy, on an airy ridge, to a superb viewpoint.

From the main camping spot, take the path due N to Hasta Hocanin Yaylası (q.v.), 1hr. (All subsequent timings are from Hasta Hocanin Yaylası.) Leaving the largest of the lakes, pass between this and another smaller lake, heading ENE.

Skirt the very foot of the crag ahead (15mins from large lake) and go up a steep rocky gully, which is an easy scramble. Keeping beneath slabs, continue skirting round the toe of the ridge to cross eventually into a subsidiary valley containing a small lake. (30mins). Ahead (N) is a pass; the route takes this.

Skirt the deep bowl beyond the small lake via its RH slopes, then easily up through a rockband (45mins), to reach the pass and ridge crest proper in 1hr. Pt 3517m is a short distance W along the easy ridge top, a further 20mins.

Continue W and either drop down easy scree to Hasta Hocanin yaylası, or continue W on scree up face to the L of the E ridge of Tosun Tepe. Towards the summit, the ridge narrows as you follow it more directly. Allow 1hr from Pt 3517m. The continuation traverse is quite a bit harder (grade III/IV), so retrace your steps in descent.

Direktaş 3510m

For such an impressive rock spire, there is a relatively easy route to the summit, which should be within the capabilities of an unroped competent scrambler

AL24 East couloir Grade II

The scree couloir which this route takes can be seen on the walk up from the Hacer Valley ; otherwise it is hidden and unsuspected when viewed from the upper Yedigöller. (NB. it is not the huge right-angled corner which forms the eastern demarcation of the North face!)

The most sensible approach is to traverse in low under the N face of Direktaş, passing Direk Göl initially, and continuing to where the eastern spur of Direktaş descends and peters out. Ascend onto the spur and follow it easily upwards to gain the now apparent scree gully ahead. This is loose (take care if ascending in a party) but not

Direktaş

difficult, and leads directly onto the summit. The views are rather disappointing, being restricted by nearby Kızılyar. Total ascent time from camp: 2-2$^{1}/_{2}$hrs. Descent: by same route.

AL25 Kızılyar 3654m

This impressive S-bounding wall of the lower Yedigöller basin provides a fine ridge route, with particularly good views of the Torasan range. Other than some easy scrambling to avoid gendarmes, the ridge is far easier than its crenellated appearance would suggest. In early season the loose screes would be hidden under snow (ice-axe essential).

From the main upper Yedigöller basin there extends a large subsidiary basin to the south, known as Latır Kırı. This is filled with substantial snowpatches until late summer and beyond. Virtually due S of the Yayla can be seen a scree spur which descends from the main ridge encircling the subsidiary basin. Head for this, keeping to the RH side (W) of the basin. Gain the toe of this ridge (45mins).

Follow the scree crest to reach bedrock (1hr 10mins). Continue in this general line, scrambling on loose scree, passing to the R of a prominent rotten rock pinnacle some 15m high. There are one or two unpleasant, though not particularly difficult, short sections before the ridge crest is reached abruptly after 1hr 30mins. Small cairn.

Follow the ridge, mainly on its RH (SE) side, initially passing an easy rock step, then skirt round the first obvious high point (or detour to top for views if time permits), heading roughly N. The ridge which runs off down to the R divides the Karagöl Valley , with Karagöl itself lying deep in the northern arm. Continuing along the main ridge, this soon angles sharply rightwards towards the ENE. This marks the start of Kızılyar proper. Climb up the ridge crest (easy) and follow this to the highest point (3hrs 15mins). A magnificent walk. Descent : via same route.

AL26 The South-bounding ridge (Pts 3610m and 3620m)

Another fine ridge expedition, with the added benefit of providing a circular route. Straightforward throughout, with some very short Grade I/II scrambling sections.

The approach is as for Kızılyar as far as the main ridge (1hr 30mins). From the small cairn, follow the ridge SSW easily. It is 20mins or so to the next top, which reveals magnificent views again of the Southern Aladağ peaks.

Keep on the ridge crest to gain another top after a further 20mins. (2hrs 10mins total). Descend the SE ridge for 50m, then diagonally R across screes. The head of the Emlı Valley lies below, with the slender column of Parmakkaya clearly visible.

Drop down for 75m (towards the Emlı Valley), then horizontally towards a rocky buttress, turn the corner, and keep traversing to the rim of a deep couloir with steep 50 degree snow which drops down towards Yedigöller. Regain the ridge, and follow this round to a huge couloir with hanging snowfields (30mins from 2nd top, 2hrs 40mins total).

Head back NNW up the ridge, which soon curves to become a W ridge. Take the easiest line, either on the crest or just to its L. 25mins beyond the big couloir, reach another cairned summit, and a view of the lower Emli Valley.

Keep just W of N along the ridge, which turns L (NW). Gain the easy-angled broad ridge, which steepens towards the top. This is deceptively long and steep!

(NB. There is a possible descent route back down to Yedigöller from the start of the broad ridge: not advisable when early season or if unequipped for snow. 40m past the low point of the ridge, head diagonally down across scree, above rock slabs and a snow lake, to a broad scree run and the valley bottom.)

From the cairned summit, retrace your steps for 2m, and descend NE down a little scree gully for 150m (care) until a traverse line leads back up to the main ridge. Either:

a)   follow this round until a fairly gentle scree slope below Kizilkaya allows an easy descent to Yedigöller, or, quicker but less pleasantly:

b)   descend diagonally from the scree gully, traversing L to a long snow patch and good glissade. 1hr 30mins descent, $4^{1}/_{2}$-5hrs round trip.

AL27 Kızılkaya 3725m

The second highest mountain in the Aladağlar, it appears impregnable when seen from Çelikbuyduran Pass. The route described here is Grade III; unfortunately, the rock is very poor in most places, necessitating great care.

From Yedigöller, head up the side basin (Latır Kırı) and ascend the obvious very broad scree slope leading up to the top of the long spur which ends in an abrupt cliff (below and in front of Kızılkaya itself).

Once on the spur, carry straight on ahead to the low point in the ridge of Kızılkaya, just to the R of a satellite top. The ridge itself is not feasible from here; cross over onto the opposite SW face of the mountain. The route continues at roughly this height, traversing the face by the easiest line, crossing one or two small descending spurs, until a slightly larger spur/gully system leads up to emerge on the ridge crest virtually at the summit. 4-5hrs from Yedigöller. Descent - via same route (3-4hrs).

AL28 Demirkazık 3756m via Yaşemin Pass Grade II

This long route is essentially the same as the standard approach from the head of the Narpuz valley; the steep Yaşemin Pass provides the connection between Narpuz and Yedigöller.

The pass involves some awkward (grade II) scrambling on the Narpuz side in late summer; in early summer steep 40 degree snow necessitates ice-axe and crampons. Rope advisable. Not suitable for backpacking!

From the campsite in Yedigöller, Yaşemin pass lies roughly NW, and is the main weakness in the ridge descending rightwards from Embler. Take the easiest line to the summit of the pass (no difficulties on this side), approx. 1hr 30mins.

The line of descent taken depends on the state of the snow; either climb down the snow or scramble down rocks, to reach the head of the Narpuz valley. Ice-axe and crampons useful, essential in early season. From here, ascend the tiresome scree to the top of the Demirkazık pass and the junction with the normal SE ridge route. ($2^1/4$-$2^1/2$hrs to valley head from Yedigöller; 4hrs to top of Demirkazık pass. Allow as long for the return journey.)

AL29 Yedigöller to Barazama

From the campsite, head towards Direk Göl, skirting it on the L. The derelict building is a mountain hut which was never completed. Pas this, and another small lake at the E toe of Direktaş - good campsite.

A well-trodden path leads down the valley, with magnificent views of Direktaş behind.

After 45mins the valley deepens and the trail drops steeply. 15mins more walking affords views of the Hacer Valley floor and the first trees. The good track winds its way down the RH side of the valley, beneath the fine N face of Ortosan 3405m (or Ortakaya). (The NW couloir looks a reasonably-angled snow ascent from here, though I know of no ascents.)

The valley bottom is alive with apollo butterflies. A small yayla of 1 or 2 tents sits just above the start of the trees; beware of dogs!

The birch trees soon give way to pine, and a second yayla is reached, where a jeep track to Barazama starts.

Kızılkaya from Yedigöller

Other onward routes from Yedigöller
From the south bounding ridge previously described (route AL26), it is possible to drop down easy scree into either the Karagöl or upper Emlı valleys.

For both routes, good weather is advisable due to the high, exposed nature of the ridge. This is suitable for experienced backpackers only.

The Vay-Vay/Torasan area

This is the least visited part of the Aladağ range, largely due to the problems of access. These can be overcome, though, and the determined walker will be rewarded with some of the most spectacular scenery in the region. The fine rock peaks of Torasan, Vay-Vay, Boruklu, and a host of other unnamed mountains lend this area a distinct character of its own.

The area is defined by two valleys with a range of peaks between them; the northernmost valley is the Karagöl Valley, the southern one is the Kokorot Valley. Of these, the Kokorot Valley is much the more suitable for ascending of peaks, via their more gentle southern flanks. There is a high, though easy, pass between the two valleys in their upper reaches.

I have walked in the valleys here, but have not climbed any of the peaks. I entered this area at the end of my last trip to the Aladag - in retrospect I wish I had come here first. Consequently, I have not been able to give route descriptions for any peaks.

Approaches

From the West
The quickest way is to walk in via the Emlı Valley, and cross via the pass S of Cebelbaşı described in route AL19 into the Kokorot Valley.

From Yedigöller
(Yedigöller can be reached from E or W.) This means of approach involves gaining the south bounding ridge of Yedigöller as described in route AL26. From this ridge, at a point a short way beyond Pt 3625m, it is possible to descend the long scree slope down into the upper Kokorot Valley. Other than the short scrambling on the ascent to the ridge, this route presents no problems. It is at a high altitude, though, and an eye needs to be kept on the weather.

It is also possible to drop down off the ridge much earlier and descend to the Karagöl Valley.

From the East
Not including the Yedigöller approach, there are two alternatives: either gaining the Karagöl Valley from Barazama, then crossing over to the Kokorot Valley, or walking to Acıman (see route AL35) and approaching from there.

From the South
From Acıman, follow route AL35 as far as the un-named yayla 1hr 15mins above Acıman. This lies at the foot of the Kokorot Valley. Continue up the valley, which is unmistakable, with fine peaks on either side.

Bases
Kokorot Valley:
In common with much of the Southern Aladağ, there are not many springs here. There is a good spring just down and S of the pass over from from Emlı Valley. It is located due N of Sulağankaya, a peak on the south-west bounding ridge, which itself casts a ridge down into the valley. This also provides a reasonable campsite.

Karagöl Valley:
By Karagöl itself is the obvious place to camp.

AL30 Karagöl to Kokorot

A useful route, it allows the trekker to see both valleys without taking the time-consuming approach via Acıman.
From Karagöl, head SW over the ridge in the valley, then head back SE to skirt the spur which descends from the main south bounding ridge of the Karagöl Valley. Once round this, an obvious pass is visible to the SW, and W of the summit of Boruklu. Attain this pass over easy scree, and descend easily down the far side into the Kokorot Valley. 3-4hrs.

Barazama to Acıman
The normal way of reaching Acıman from Barazama passes via the spectacular emergent rivers at Şelale, and is well worth the dogleg

this involves. This route is described first. Some road walking is unavoidable, but footpaths are taken where they exist. As Şelale is such a spectacular place, it is worth spending a night there rather than in Barazama.

AL31 Via Selale

From Barazama, follow the main road, roughly SSW, out of the village, passing the forestry office. Where the road skirts a low ridge ahead, a path takes a direct shortcut through the notch. The road is soon regained by a large cemetery. At the end of this cemetery, take a path diagonally L, down through fields to cross the river (40mins from Barazama) at a wooden bridge. This is a pleasant spot for swimming.

Follow the bulldozed track, which is unused due to rockfall. Where it turns back R, there is a good track which traverses the steep scree ahead. (This is difficult to find.) This leads shortly to an attractive meadow dotted with low animal shelters.

At the end of the meadow, cross the river again by a rickety log bridge, or wade the ford, up to the road on the other side. This is followed to **Kapuzbası**, a small village with attractive stilted extensions to the houses. Facilities are limited to a telephone and post office.

A further 15mins along the road, the valley narrows considerably, and as one turns the corner, the first of Şelale's magnificent cascades is seen. There are some quaint watermills here, and the beginnings of some tourist facilities in the shape of a few picnic benches covered in awnings. Sometimes there is someone selling fish here, sometimes not. A few hundred metres downstream, three full rivers gush clear from the rock. This fabulous display is still too remote to feature on any package tour itinerary, and hopefully will remain so. There is a camping spot by the watermills, but the best option is to continue along the road for a further 15-20mins to the little village of Şelale (the name means "waterfall"), situated at the end of the valley narrows, where another tributary comes in from the right (2³/₄-3hrs from Barazama).

The village must surely rank as one of the most idyllic in Turkey. Nearly all the houses are built on stilts in amongst the trees, and the

The spectacular emergent rivers at Şelale

cliffs beyond have several small streams spouting forth. The main street has a stream flowing down it, which also powers the small watermills. Several open shelters on stilts are available for sleeping - just ask the locals where is best.

There is a small Bakkaliye, and, as one would expect with such an abundance of water, plenty of fish and fresh produce available.

AL32 Şelale to Acıman

From the centre of the village, head upstream, following the tributary, in a westerly direction. Pass a prominent isolated rock, keeping on the path, which is overarched with vines after 40mins. Switchback briefly up the tractor track, and follow this along the river bank.

The tractor trail gradually disintegrates, and after 1hr 15mins, where the track continues on the L bank (true R), cross via a small log footbridge, and steeply up a trail on the opposite bank. The trail soon levels off, then climbs steeply again on a good zigzag track, crossing an old road (2hrs). Clearly visible is a newly-cut road; stay on the footpath up to several houses set in fields, with the new track just behind them.

Cross the new road, and follow the ridge upwards, beside pasture, to enter the pines. This section is very hot in midsummer, but there are good views back down the valley to Şelale village. Continue to a clearing with a white tent, and a road just beyond - follow this L. It is easy to go astray on this section - keep on the RH side of the main valley, and aim towards the lower wooded ridge and col on the R side of the valley. There are many dirt roads hereabouts. Eventually the road you are on levels out onto a grassy meadow. Where the road bends L, take a path straight on to reach the gap a few hundred metres ahead on the skyline.

Cross barbed wire at the top, and emerge onto a road and a view of the southern Aladağlar. Leave this road after 25m, for a track down L. (4hrs 30mins.) A hut visible down below is used by Trek Travel as a base. The valley you are now in is a beautiful place, full of bird and insect life in summer. There have been some commendable attempts at re-afforestation here. Acıman itself lies just beyond the ridge at the L head of this valley.

Follow the dirt road up the valley, passing occasional beekeepers'

Beekeeper and family, Acıman yayla

tents, to a gate. The road leads round to Acıman; it is more pleasant and quicker if walking to cross the valley bottom and up the other side to join the road at the skyline col. (NB. A prominent road skirts round on the R. There is a prominent wedge-shaped rock c.30m high on the skyline - aim well to the L of this.)

Arrive to overlook another small subsidiary valley (5hrs 15mins); Acıman is on the other side of this. This area consists of impervious rock, with the occasional limestone boulder outcrop. There are one or two yayla tents here, but the main interest lies in the abundance of butterflies; I've never seen such a variety or number elsewhere in Turkey.

The road leads in 15mins across this valley to the next col, overlooking Acıman. Take the L fork down to Acıman, which is reached in a further 15mins (5³/₄-6hrs in total)

AL33 Direct route from Barazama to Acıman

It is possible to ascend from the mouth of the Karagöl Valley to the Aciman plateau, affording a considerable time saving.

The route utilises the same approach as for the Karagöl Valley. From Barazama, take the wide side valley, heading SW, passing several Yaylas, to the mouth of an obvious deep valley/gorge. This leads up to Karagöl. Instead of following this, keep on the mountain (R) side of the valley you are in, to reach the valley head very shortly. There is a track which heads steeply up the back wall, suddenly to emerge onto a broad, sloping grassy plateau - the upper part of the subsidiary valley before Acıman. (4hrs 30mins.)

Contour across this, then descend slightly to gain the dirt road which is taken by the previous route, 30mins before Acıman. (6hrs total from Barazama.)

AL34 Barazama to Karagöl Valley

This approach leads you to the remote and less visited southern peaks. Karagöl cannot be described as an ideal base for their ascents, however, lying separated from them by an intervening ridge. It is nevertheless an attractive high mountain valley, and can be combined with other routes to form part of a hard circuit of the range.

Barazama offers the only easy approach to Karagöl Valley. From Barazama, take the wide side valley heading SW, passing several Yaylas, to the mouth of an obvious deep valley/gorge. Follow this in its entirety to gain the lake of Karagöl. (7hrs)

AL35 Acıman via Auçiveli pass to Emli Valley

This route does not fit easily with the area classification used. Its greatest attraction is as part of a circuit of the Aladağlar. The route described here takes two days; it can usefully be combined with an ascent of Alaca (3582m) via the easy E ridge route.

From Acıman the route basically heads WSW along the foot of the mountains proper. Many of the peaks look somewhat less dramatic from this aspect, but side valleys reveal tantalising glimpses of fine rock spires. This is awkward country to traverse - many intervening spurs and small valleys mean a substantial amount of up and down. This area of the Aladağ is hardly ever visited; the inhabitants of the yaylas *en route* are extremely hospitable, and curious to know what you are doing there.

Gain the obvious track through the limestone above Acıman,

passing a yayla. Emerge onto a ridge after 30mins. Ahead, there is a clearer view of the mountains. Two yaylas lie isolated in the valley. A faint, but good, track traverses the hillside near them, leading to the RH end of the low flat-topped limestone ridge ahead (1hr 15mins). (There is a good stream beyond the yayla.) From this ridge, just W of due N ahead, the very prominent conical peak is one of the southern group, probably Sulağankaya. It is difficult to say which one, exactly; the existing maps are incomplete and inaccurate in this part of the Aladağlar.

Continue traversing the next valley, and head westwards, first by dropping down. There is little option but to descend to the yayla, before traversing a steep path through the wood, which drops down to the dry river bed. Up the other side of this past a large boulder. This yayla is Çadıroğlu yayla, and is the departure point for the southern flanks of Güzeller.

The path peters out, but the going is straightforward. Gain the ridge after a long slog (3hrs from Acıman). Above (NW) is Kaldı, Alaca is virtually due W. The latter appears as little more than a slight bump on the main ridge when seen from here - the southern flanks of Alaca are very gentle in reality. The Auçiveli pass is fortunately this side of Alaca, taking the obvious, though slight, notch in the skyline ridge. As the track up to this is easily lost, it is worth memorising this.

A few hundred metres ahead is another isolated yayla; there is a good traversing track approximately 100m above the yayla.

Gain this and aim SW towards the shelf in the middle distance - the going is much more pleasant again. There is a yayla just before and below the shelf - take the path which skirts the hillside to the L (S). There is a weak spring just beyond the yayla, and an excellent one 50m further on.

In the distance to the SE can be seen a dirt road which winds right up to the top of a prominent conical hill with a small construction on top - possibly a watch tower? Down below there is a basin with a yayla and emergent stream (4hrs 15mins).

A further 20mins leads to another ridge-top yayla - this is the upper part of the ridge which leads towards the watch tower. Skirt above scattered trees. This yayla is known as Karayurt; the family here were particularly friendly, and helped revive me on a blisteringly hot day with glasses of *ayran*.

Beyond here, the path skirts the head of another valley, to reach a further spur. The valley on the other (W) side of this spur has a road running down it.

It is easy to miss the departure point for the Auçiveli pass, but looking W from the spur, a parallel spur on the other side of the valley has a prominent zigzag road contouring the hillside, and another road beyond which climbs right to the top of the ridge.

The Auçiveli route starts just by the former; if you have reached the latter road, you have gone too far. A useful landmark for finding the start of the path up to the pass is a greenish rock scar/quarry and a road that appears to peter out at it. The path starts up the main (N) hillside just by this. Initially, the route up to the pass follows a right-kinking narrows, which then widens out into a broad scree slope. The scree slope leads easily up to the summit of the Auçiveli pass (4hrs from Karayurt).

If you are tired or do not wish for a high camp, then staying at Karayurt is the best option.

Gaining the summit of the pass you are rewarded with fine views towards the western flanks of the Aladağ. Both Kaldı and Alaca are easy (Grade II) ascents from here via the W and E ridges respectively, taking 3hrs for the former and 2-2$^{1}/_{2}$hrs return to the col for the latter. (See "excursions from Emli Valley" routes AL10 and AL13.)

Descending from the Auçiveli pass down towards the Emli Valley, one can expect to encounter steep snow in early season, but this has usually receded sufficiently by early July to allow an easy descent.

The barren cwm below offers several flattish areas for camping, and meltwater springs. Continuing down, the valley bends to the R, and affords occasional glimpses of Kaldı. It forms a shallow, snow-filled basin, which drops away steeply at its end. From here, the first view of the spectacular rock spire, Parmakkaya, is obtained. Depending upon the amount of snow, a fast descent can be made down the basin.

Carry on down the valley, passing Parmakkaya. Directly ahead can be seen Karasay, **3472m**, with the obvious scree slope ascent. Just below Parmakkaya, set well to the L of the path, lies the elusive Akşampınarı. As the name literally translates as "night spring", it is unwise to rely on finding this for a water source. It makes more sense to continue down for another 30mins to the main Emlı Valley bottom, where there is water by the large yayla at the foot of this side valley. (Total descent time from Auçiveli pass: $1^3/_4$-2hrs.)

From here a choice of routes either leads directly down the Emlı Valley towards Çamardı or Çukurbağ (dirt track), or ascending the spur on the RH entrance to the valley and contouring round to Sokullupınar (as described in reverse from Sokullupınar, route AL4).

Multi-day tours of the Aladağlar

Numerous options exist, and the proximity of contrasting areas make the Aladağlar ideal for this. A few suggested itineraries are included below. These are easily varied depending on time available. I haven't included peaks in the circuit; again, this is up to you.

1) A hard circuit, starting and finishing at Çukurbağ
   Çukurbağ - Sokullupınar - Cımbar Deresı - Dipsiz Göl- Yıldız Göl - Yedigöller - S-bounding ridge to Karagöl - Barazama - Şelale - Açiman - Auçiveli pass - Emlı Valley - Çukurbağ. This "grand tour" covers all the main areas and sights, and would take a fit walker 9 to 11 days. It can be finished at Barazama or Acıman.

2) The classic traverse.
   Çukurbağ - Yalak Deresı - Çelikbuyduran - Yedigöller - Barazama - Şelale
   5 to 6 days, with only one arduous day.

3) A southern traverse
   Çukurbağ - Sokullupınar - Emlı Valley - Kokorot Valley - Karagöl Valley - Barazama
   5 days.

PART SEVEN

The Bolkar Toros

Introduction

This fine range of mountains is the western continuation of the main Taurus chain from the Aladağlar, and lies separated from the latter range by the deep notch known as the Cilician Gates.

Unlike the Aladağlar, these mountains are more typical of the Taurus as a whole, consisting of long limestone ridges, high plateaux and lakes, and deeply cut valleys. There are no spectacular peaks as in the Aladağlar, but numerous points over 3000m, with Medetsiz at 3524m the highest mountain. As a whole, the area is little frequented by trekkers, and those that do visit tend to cover much the same ground. This is a pity, as it is a vast, complex area, particularly on the southern flanks. I myself am guilty of this failing, having made only a very brief exploratory visit. This, then, is the route described, although I would commend the area to anyone with a desire to get off the beaten track. There are a wealth of walks just waiting to be done, and it would be perfectly possible to spend the whole holiday here. The complexity of the southern slopes, with their deep gorges, mean that it is far easier to start treks from the North. The trek described starts from the village of **Darboğaz**.

Approaches

From Niğde, Konya, Ankara or Adana, catch a bus to the town of Ulukışla (1428m). This is situated at the major junction on the northern side of the Cilician Gates, where the Konya/Ankara and Kayseri roads to Adana meet. Consequently, it is a very easy place to reach. Stock up here before catching a bus to the village of Darbogaz, approx. 15km SE.

Ulukışla, incidentally, has one of the most magnificent of all Turkish caravanserai. Under no circumstances should you miss seeing this. Despite its size, it is not signposted and easy to overlook - ask *Kervanseray nerede, lütfen?*

Maps

There is a 1:25,000 scale map to the area produced by Bozkurt Ergor (see introduction).

A traverse of the range

Darboğaz to Karagöl

Looking S from Darboğaz, there are three streams in separate valleys which converge near the village. The route described follows the LH, most easterly, stream which runs in a S-SSE direction.

To attain this valley, head S through orchards, to follow a path alongside the stream. There are several paths following the various tributaries, which can be a bit confusing, but essentially you follow the main valley to where it starts to curve R (westwards), then follow the LH branch roughly due S. This leads up onto a grassy ridge which runs along the side of the valley in a NE-SW direction. 2hrs 15mins.

A dirt track parallels the ridge, then drops down into the Arpalık valley some way downstream. At the valley head, where you are now, is a grassy area with several springs (possible camping spot).

From here, keep heading just W of S along a path which leads up through a narrow neck near a stream to emerge at the beautiful lake of Karagöl (c.2600m). 3hrs from Darboğaz. There is nice camping to be had on the springy turf by the lake - an idyllic spot.

Exploring around Karagöl

Before moving on to climb Medetsiz, it may be worth spending a day around Karagöl. Heading SW up the valley brings one to the equally beautiful Çini Gol (lit. "Tile Lake") after 10mins. The name derives from the colour, which under certain lighting conditions has the same turquoise hue as the famous Iznik tiles.

Above the lake, in a SSW direction, is the pass of Kara Gedik. This is a further 45mins walk away, but is well worth the effort for the view, which can be improved upon by continuing along the ridge in either direction.

The Kara Gedik itself (3000m) leads down into the southern valleys of the range, and eventually down to the plains around Tarsus. This would provide an interesting trip, not too adventurous.

Karagöl to Medetsiz 3524m

The way described is the most direct way to climb Medetsiz from Karagöl, and gives a long but rewarding day. There are few tracks to speak of over most of the route, and the going is rocky.

From Karagöl, the peak of Tahtakaya, 3372m, lies virtually due E. This marks the northernmost point of a large bowl; our route heads for the SE corner. Aim ESE from Karagöl, up into the bowl. A tiring slog up the slopes leads to the main ridge in 1hr 30mins. Aim for the point on the ridge where the spur to Tahtakaya meets the main E-W Bolkar ridge (crossed by the Kara Gedik). Basically, this ridge is followed in its entirety to reach the summit of Medetsiz. Armed only with a map, I wasn't sure if there was meant to be a path. Depending on your scrambling ability, you may need to drop down on either side of the ridge crest on tiring scree slopes. The only point where you may go wrong is shortly after attaining the main ridge. It curves round towards the N and Kızıldokot - make sure you take this, rather than the S-trending ridge to Kesif Dag, 3475m. Shortly after this junction, however, you do take the SE-heading ridge which quickly curves back E and leads to Medetsiz proper. I took around 4hrs from Karagöl to the summit of Medetsiz, travelling light.

The view from the summit is extensive, haze permitting. The Aladağlar are prominent to the NE, and, if lucky, Erciyes Dağ way to the N.

Descent from Medetsiz

From the summit, I retraced my line of ascent, taking around 3hrs to reach Karagöl, then back to Darboğaz. By all accounts, though, descending the mountain to the N and heading out through the Horoz valley is the most popular itinerary. Rather than carry packs over the tiresome screes to the summit of Medetsiz, it is normal to backtrack from Karagöl. Return to the roadhead and follow a path down the attractive Arpalık valley to the village of Maden. From here, a path leads SSE over a high ridge to a high basin running parallel to, and just N of, the watershed ridge. This place is known as Yalaklar, and there is a spring hereabouts.

Camp here, and a path leads up to the summit of Medetsiz, to the

SW. This is in fact the normal route of ascent. In descent from Yalaklar, follow the basin down, then the Kızıltepe ridge on the L (N) of the valley where it drops away steeply. Drop down again to the river, which leads to Horoz village and the main Cilician Gates road to Adana.

Alternative exit via Kocagedik 3100m

From the point at where you follow the Kızıltepe ridge along the N side of the steepening valley, it is possible to head SSE and skirt around the upper section of the valley (before it steepens). Then head due E, diagonally across the hillside, to gain the ancient Kocagedik (pass). Dropping down this on the S side leads to the Elmalı gorge, and 4hrs beyond there, the village of Tekir on the main Cilician Gates road.

PART EIGHT

The Western Toros

Introduction

For the purposes of this book, the Western Toros is taken to be the continuation of the range west from the Bolkar Toros as far as the Aegean coastal plain.

In character the Western Toros resemble the Bolkar and continuations eastward, being arid limestone ridges. They are slightly lower, attaining a maximum height of a little over 3000m, and their flanks are more wooded and greener, particularly on the southern, Mediterranean, slopes.

West of Antalya, the Toros descend to the coast in a series of ridges running roughly NE-SW, terminating abruptly to form the spectacular coastline of this area.

For the walker, this is an area of abundant choice, where you can quickly cross from barren upland to forested valley and fertile meadow. The contrast between developed coast and traditional interior is nowhere more marked than in this region. I have only described one peak in detail, to give an indication of what is to be found; the reader is left to explore the area more fully themselves.

Akdağ 3016m

One of many similar southern Toros mountains, Akdağ 3016m is a high point on a limestone ridge. Close to the tourist traps of Fethiye and Ölü Deniz, it offers anyone holidaying here an opportunity to experience the scenery and lifestyle of the high Toros. Besides the mountain, the remarkable gorge of Saklikent, and several classical sites nearby, make this a very worthwhile excursion.

Approaches and route description
From Fethiye or Kemer, take a minibus direct to Arsa Köyu. (1hr 30mins journey from Fethiye.) Akdağ dominates the view here, above the village. This is an attractive spot, with pine trees, cultivated fields and many beehives.

The next stage is to reach the small village of Palamut yaylası, 16km distant via a dirt road. Either take a taxi, or as I did, hire a lift on the back of a motorbike (£5), to reach there.

From here there are a whole series of peaks, and whilst it is perfectly possible to climb Akdağ in a long day, this is a fine area in which to spend a few days backpacking and exploring. (S of the village, Duman Dağ is the peak on the other side of the deep Tocak gorge. It has a fine view from its summit.)

A few hundred metres past the cafe in Palamut, where the main road takes a LH bend - a steeper forestry road goes off L. Follow this for about 3.5km, keeping to the steeper tracks on the R- don't go to the low cultivated ridge on the skyline. The terrain is beautiful, being thin pasture land dotted with spruce and cedar. The road peters out around here.

Follow a ridge between higher ridges up towards a wooded hill - bear R, on a good track. There is a spring down L of the ridge top.

30mins from the road head, pass several pine trees with hacked-away bases - the resin-rich wood has been taken for fire-starting. Continue along the valley by a stream for 5mins, then more steeply up to a fine viewpoint of Akdağ. The route ahead is now obvious, following the skyline ridge to the distant summit. Directly ahead is a large stony cwm of red rock, largely devoid of vegetation.

10-15mins from the viewpoint lead up to the top of a tree-covered hill, past a summer encampment. The cliffs ahead are avoided by a slope on the L to gain the ridge proper. 1hr 45mins from Palamut.

The ridge leads directly now to the bare summit, a further 3hrs distant; no chance of route-finding error.

Returning from Akdağ, make every effort to visit the remarkable Saklıkent (also known as Ulu Pinar or "great spring"). Situated 30mins by dirt road from Arsu Köyu, Saklıkent lies at the mouth of the great Tocak gorge which splits the SE end of the Akdağ ridge. Considering its location, close to the coastal resorts, it is surprising this site is not better known.

Saklıkent, which translates as "Hidden city" is reached via a rickety wooden bridge at the gorge mouth, where it debouches onto the flat river plain. An iron walkway leads across the sheer walls, just above the raging river.

The walkway continues for 100m, to where the gorge opens out.

Here, springs emerge from the walls with incredible force. There is an improbably-situated bar on the other side of the river, with a few tables outside. At its highest, the gorge is around 500m deep, and stretches back for 17km.

Across from the bar, a tottering ladder leads up to a large cave, an ancient dwelling.

To leave Saklıkent, follow the road on the L bank of the river downstream. This eventually emerges onto the main road, passing the ancient amphitheatre of Tlos.

PART NINE

Erciyes Dağ

History

Erciyes Dağ 3917m is an extinct volcano which rises in splendid isolation from the central Anatolian plain, near the city of Kayseri. Its graceful form, and the contrast it offers with the surrounding plateau mean that Erciyes has been invested with a spiritual dimension, similar to Ararat. Known to the Hellenics as Mount Argaeus, it must have been a familiar landmark to caravans on the trade routes across Asia Minor. Recently, a summer thaw exposed a 2000yr old Roman temple, hidden for centuries under ice, near the summit. Zoroastrians also regarded this as a sacred summit.

In modern times, it has become a centre for skiing, as well as being a popular climbing venue. Snow-capped throughout the year, the lower slopes are rather austere, being barren and treeless.

In common with several other Turkish volcanoes, the apparently simple conical shape belies a rather complex summit geography, with several satellite peaks and hidden basins.

Unlike most similar peaks, however, Erciyes Dağ involves technical climbing to reach the highest point. This consists of steep rock, none too solid.

Approaches

From Kayseri, a good road (signposted in yellow) leads S to the Kayak Evi ("ski house"), 26km distant. The only public transport to here is during the ski season; outside these times it is necessary to take a taxi from Kayseri, around £6. Stock up in Kayseri.

High altitude means that the winter season is long and severe - late spring (May, June) is probably the ideal time to ascend. At this time, there is still a decent snow covering, lessening the amount of scree to be crossed.

Maps

Bozkurt Ergor has produced a 1:25,000 map of the area; a copy of

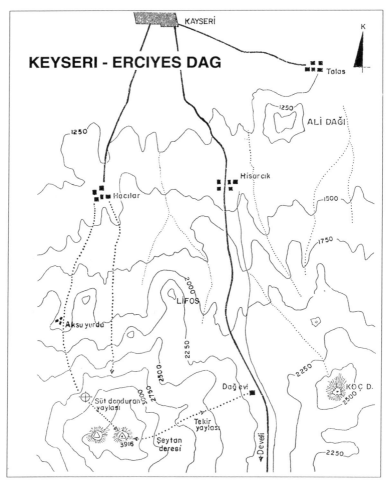

KEYSERI - ERCIYES DAG

this is available (on a smaller scale) from the tourist information office. Beware - this may be laterally compressed, making N-S travel seem much faster than E-W!

There is an old map, dated 1934/35, by Dr Bartsch, Hannover. Scale 1:200,000.

Route description

Tekir Yaylası has several hotels, the Kayak Evi ("ski house") and an ugly "sport building" - this is not one of Turkey's beauty spots. These offer accommodation throughout the year, and are worth considering if you arrive here late. Otherwise, follow the ski pylons uphill to where they end. Continue heading directly upslope (roughly E) for 1hr to reach a high cwm, where there is a rough camping spot at c.3000m. There is an intermittent spring here, just N of the camping spot.

There are two choices for prospective summiteers; either retracing one's steps back to Kayak Evi, or continuing over the mountain to descend to the village of Soğutlupınar. The former choice reduces the amount of backpacking necessary.

High Camping spot to summit 3917m

On the southern side of the cwm, and curving round to the highest summit Pt 3917, is a long, gentle ridge. Follow this, avoiding difficulties by descending on either side, to reach the rocks that form Pt 3917. This is the furthest of the summits reached when traversing the ridge from this direction. The final rock tower is grade III, loose. The way is marked by several pegs in situ. Abseil descent. 4-5 hrs from campsite, 3hrs 30mins descent.

If continuing the traverse, due NW of the summit are two small buildings at c.2750m altitude. These are respectively a ruined hut and a partly-built one that is unlikely ever to be finished. From below the summit rocks, head N along a ridge which curves around to the L (W). Descend down this to gain the two huts, which are off to the R across a gully.

From the lower, older of the two huts, head NNE along a dirt track, until a water pumping station is reached ahead. This is known as Aksuyurdu, and from here the path continues straight down through meadows to reach a good dirt road.

This in turn leads through a rocky defile to reach a quarried area. There is a spring here, known as Sogutlupınar. 2hrs from ruined huts.

Keep heading down until you reach a junction on the good road. 1hr from Sogutlupınar. Take the RH turn, and after 30mins, reach the small town of Hacılar. Buses from here to Kayseri are frequent. 9hrs total from camping spot.

PART TEN

Other Areas

Uludağ

One of the most popular of Turkish mountains, Uludağ is situated
on the outskirts of Bursa, and consequently affords the residents of
Istanbul access to real mountains.

Despite the surrounding terrain, Uludağ is a substantial
mountain. 2543m high, it catches more than its fair share of bad
weather. In winter Uludağ is a major ski centre, in summer a
popular venue for family outings.

Along with several other mountains on the Mediterranean
littoral, Uludağ was known as Olympos in ancient times. In later
times it served as a refuge for Christian hermits.

Uludağ would make a fitting end to a Turkish holiday, and is
highly recommended. Take the ferry from Istanbul across the Sea of
Marmara to Bursa, the former capital of the Ottoman empire. This
beautiful city with its green-tiled mosque is well worth the visit.

Being so close to the urban centres is reflected in Uludağ's
tourist facilities. In contrast to other Turkish mountains Uludağ has
marked trails, there is a basic sketch map available, and there is even
a cable-car to take you part way.

Starting points
From Bursa, there are two options.

Firstly, take a minibus to Karabelen, 22km distant. This is an
entry gate to the Uludağ Milli Park (National Park), and from here
roads continue E to Kirazlıyayla ("Cherry yayla") and an area of
hotels, known prosaically as Oteller, 5km or so from the park
entrance.

Alternatively, the cable-car (Teleferik) from near the University
leads up to Sarıalan, a short way below the hotels. The cable-car is
very busy in summer, with long queues, but is a novelty and is quite
cheap.

From the upper cable-car terminus at Sarıalan, follow the power cables, which eventually becomes a trail proper with yellow waymarks, to Oteller. Allow 1hr 45mins.

Summit 2543m from Oteller

An easy walk, with some surprising alpine scenery. In an area that contains hotels, a Tungsten mine and ski-lifts, it is nonetheless very easy to forget all this as you walk through high meadows or past glacial lakes.

To reach the summit, follow the dirt road which leads eastwards to reach the Tungsten mine. From here, head due S to gain the main ridge crest just W of the subsidiary peak, Pt 2496m at a col. 2hrs from Oteller.

From here on, you basically head SSE along this ridge to gain the summit. 2hrs from gaining crest to summit.

Whilst the summit is, needless to say, an attraction, the alpine lakes around here are worth a visit. To reach these, backtrack from the summit for 20mins to where an obvious path cuts back R (N). Follow this, waymarked, to reach a lake after 40mins. This is known as Aynalıgöl.

Having wandered around here in the mist, I was unable to locate any other lakes, but Turkish friends told me I had missed the most impressive, Karagöl. By all accounts, this is quite close, being further E and at a similar altitude. Good luck to anyone visiting this area.

In good weather, any of the lakes around here would make idyllic camping sites, and a good base for further exploration.

Nemrut Dağ

Situated above the upper headwaters of the river Kahta, which feed into the Euphrates, this mountain has become synonymous with the East of Turkey. Its summit is famous as the temple of Antiochus, a Commagene king from 64-38BC.

A series of colossal stone statues flank either side of the summit cone, itself man-made of broken stones. Over the centuries, the heads of the statues have toppled, and now lie scattered on the ground beneath. It is a unique site, which remarkably stayed undiscovered until quite recently.

Nemrut Dağ (upper Mesopotamia)

Such an archaeological remain may well have languished in obscurity were it not for the road which has been constructed to within a stone's throw of the summit. This has allowed tourists easy access to the site, and nowadays Nemrut Dağ is high on any visitor's itinerary.

For the walker, there exists an alternative route to the summit which passes through some spectacular scenery, both wild and of archaeological interest.

Starting point

The best starting point is the small town of Kâhta, 35km east of Adiyaman. This is where all the tours from the southern side of the mountain start. There are several hotels here.

The trek starting point is from the village of Eski Kâhta, some 24km further N along a dirt road. To reach this, there are several choices: either take one of the two or three daily dolmuses from town, hire a taxi, or negotiate a lift part-way with one of the tour groups driving to the summit of the mountain.

A few kilometres before Eski Kâhta, you cross a beautiful Roman bridge which spans the Kâhta river at the point where it debouches from a narrow gorge.

Eski Kâhta itself is spectacularly situated, near a narrow gorge crowned with a Mameluk castle, and crossed by a seljuk bridge. There are one or two very basic, but pleasant, rest-houses in the village where you can stay.

To reach the summit of Nemrut Dağ, allow yourself an early start and a full day's walking. Take the old road through the gorge, then simply follow the well-used path which cuts up R from the river, generally heading ENE, to reach the summit area and the crowds. When I walked up here in 1986, I confess that I didn't take much notice of the directions, but remember it being easy enough to find the way.

Once at the summit, there is a cafe and a small dormitory should you choose to stay up here and experience the sunrise next day. Alternatively, it is usually very easy to hitch a lift (possibly paying a small sum) back down to Kâhta or Eski Kâhta.

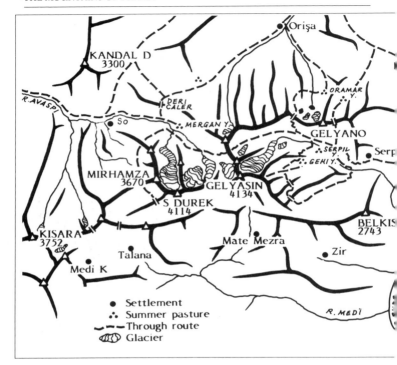

The Munzur range

Lying 50km to the west of Erzincan, this beautiful area consists of limestone mountains which reach a height of 3500m. In the central part of the range, many small lakes and high pastures provide a summer home for the local Kurds, seeking refuge from the intense heat of the valleys below. The northern part of the range, overlooking the Kemer valley, is riven by numerous deep gorges, which provide an exciting way into the mountains.

Unfortunately, Kurdish separatists, the PKK, are active in this area. Tunceli province, in which the southern half of the range lies, is under martial law. The gorges and mountains offer refuge to the PKK, and consequently any stranger walking here is likely to be

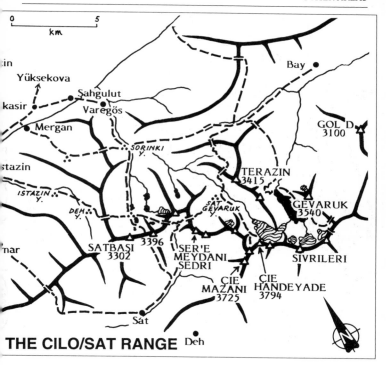

THE CILO/SAT RANGE Deh

treated with suspicion, to say the least.

In conclusion, therefore, I cannot recommend the Munzur range unless or until the political problems subside.

In the event of this occurring, the starting points for treks are: South side - Ovacik, reached via Tunceli (70km, buses £1, twice daily). North side - Alp and Kemer, reached from Erzincan.

The Cilo-Sat range

Considered by many who have visited to be Turkey's finest mountain range, these mountains lie in the far south-eastern corner of the country, in the mainly Kurdish Hâkkari province. Strictly speaking, they are two separate ranges, the Cilo and Sat, but are usually

171

treated as one in the literature. High mountains of over 4000m, residual glaciers and impressive north faces are the physical characteristics of an area that is also rich in wildlife, being home to brown bear, chamois and mouflon. It is an extraordinarily isolated mountain range, abutting onto the plains of northern Iraq, and bounded on its northern side by the deep Zap river canyon. It has developed its own unique culture, in marked contrast to anywhere else in Turkey.

Whilst this may sound intriguing, there is unfortunately a problem. This is the heartland of the Kurdish PKK, who have been waging war with the Turkish authorities for many years. When I visited the area in the mid-eighties, the situation was very tense and it was inadvisable to enter the mountains. Since then, the situation has deteriorated, the whole area has been placed off-limits to foreigners, and there seems little chance of this restriction being lifted. Even if the authorities were to relax the ban, a visitor would almost certainly encounter problems with locals. Armed robbery and kidnapping are just two possibilities. There has been talk in the papers recently of the PKK seeking to institute their own passport system for anyone wishing to visit the Southeast. Clearly, in the current climate, it would be foolhardy in the extreme to consider visiting the area. If the situation ever changes, then climbers will no doubt start exploring the region again, but detailed description of routes etc. in this book are at the moment superfluous. Consequently, I only intend to give a very brief outline of the area.

Approaches

To reach the more northern Cilo range, there are two choices - either Hakkâri or the small town of Yüksekova.

From Hakkâri, backtrack along the main Van road to the police checkpoint at Zap Karakolu, down in the main Zap canyon. A side valley, the Beyazsu, leads SE into the heart of the range.

Alternatively, from Yüksekova, head W on a rough road to Orisa Zoma, a small village which gives access to the range.

For the Sat range, a road leads from Yüksekova to Kamişlik, Yeşiltaş, and Dağlıca (the latter town having an impressive ruined church). All three afford access to the Sat range.

Kurdish village houses, Uludere

Maps

A map is rumoured to be in production by Turkish mountaineers but when or if it will ever get published is anyone's guess.

Sidney Nowill (see bibliography) refers to the possible existence of a 1:50,000 army map of the area, which is understandably not available.

As mentioned in the introduction, this area still has residual glaciers - the furthest south in western Asia. The peaks are limestone, the highest being Gelyasin (Uludoruk, Reşko Tepesı) 4135m and Buzul 4116m in the Cilo range and those around Bay Golu in the Sat range, c.3711m. Any prospective visitors should consult the literature, and possibly get in touch with the TDF for further information.

APPENDIX

List of routes described

Kackar

K39	Gungormez Dağ
K40	Samisdal trek
K41	Verçenik area - approach from N
K42	Approach from S - Çoruh valley
K43	Verçenik from Ortaköy campsite
K44	Germaniman
K45	Onwards to Pokut and Çoruh valley

Aladağlar:

AL1	Çukurbağ to Sokullupınar
AL2	Sokullupınar to Narpuz gorge
AL2A	The Dipsiz vadı
AL3	Sokullupınar to Cımbar Valley and Dipsiz Göl
AL4	Sokullupınar to Emlı Valley
AL5	Demirkazık village to Dipsiz Göl
AL6	Demirkazık E ridge
AL7	Dipsiz Göl to Yıldız Göl and Tekkekalesı
AL7A	Continuation to Pt 3517m and Yedıgöller
AL8	Emlı Valley from Çukurbağ
AL9	Auçiveli Pass from Emlı Valley
AL10	Alaca E ridge
AL11	Alaca W ridge
AL12	Un-named peak c.3100m
AL13	Kaldı W ridge
AL14	Güzeller SW ridge
AL15	Güzeller E face
AL16	Sıyırmalık
AL17	Cebelbaşı-Gürtepe ridge
AL18	Karasay (with continuation to Eznevit)
AL19	Emlı Valley to Kokorot Valley
AL20	Sokullupınar via Çelikbuyduran pass to Yedigöller
AL21	Barazama via Hacer Valley to Yedigöller
AL22	The traverse of Embler
AL23	Pt 3517m (with continuation to Tosun Tepe)
AL24	Direktaş E couloir
AL25	Kızılyar
AL26	The S-bounding ridge
AL27	Kızılkaya
AL28	Demirkazık via Yaşemin pass
AL29	Yedigöller to Barazama
AL30	Karagöl to Kokorot
AL31	Barazama (to Acıman via) to Şelale
AL32	Şelale to Acıman
AL33	Direct route Barazama to Acıman
AL34	Barazama to Karagöl Valley
AL35	Acıman via Auçiveli pass to Emli Valley

Printed by CARNMOR PRINT & DESIGN
95-97 LONDON ROAD, PRESTON, LANCASHIRE, UK.